T0104125

THE
POWER
of ONE
PRAYER

Devotional Inspiration for Women

ANITA
HIGMAN

MARIAN
LESLIE

BARBOUR
PUBLISHING

Print ISBN 978-1-63609-844-9
Adobe Digital Edition (.epub) 978-1-63609-939-2

Cover Design: Greg Jackson, Thinkpen Design

Published by Barbour Publishing, Inc., 1810 Barbour Drive, Uhrichsville, Ohio 44683, www.barbourbooks.com

Our mission is to inspire the world with the life-changing message of the Bible.

Printed in China.

To Hannah Ricks,
a young woman of beauty,
delight, and talent, but most of all,
a prayerful young woman full
of the light and love of Christ!
ANITA HIGMAN

For Sharon H.,
and all the times she lifted
us kids up to God.
It was worth it!
MARIAN LESLIE

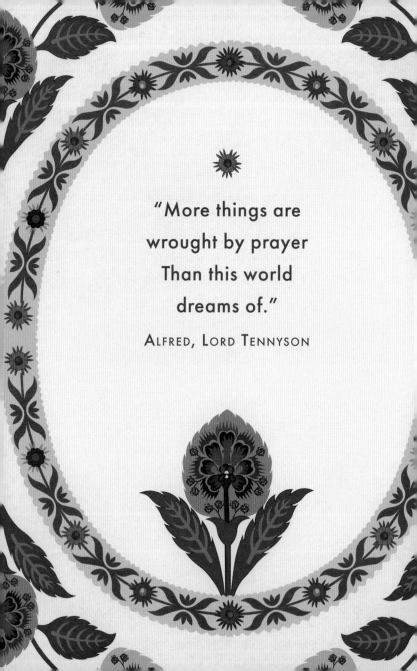

"More things are
wrought by prayer
Than this world
dreams of."

ALFRED, LORD TENNYSON

INTRODUCTION

When you talk to God, do you expect a miracle? The fact that we, as fallen creatures, can always expect an answer to our prayers from the God of the universe—whether it be a "yes" or a "no" or a "wait"—is a miracle in itself. Prayer is a supernatural communication with the Creator of all things, but it is also a profoundly intimate exchange.

We are assured in God's Word that He loves us with a passionate earnestness, an attentive love that we cannot fathom, and yet we seem determined to follow our own path no matter how dangerous or deadly. It is often in the darkest places that we long for the arms of the one who loves us, who made us. No matter where we are, in prayer, our hearts run home to God. Where they belong.

Shall we begin that journey with God—that intimate journey called prayer?

We live in the bold confidence that God hears our voices when we ask for things that fit His plan.
1 JOHN 5:14 VOICE

A BIT OF A TOAD

"I no longer call you servants, because a servant does not know his master's business. Instead, I have called you friends."
JOHN 15:15

A good friendship takes time, effort, and sensitivity, but a healthy friendship is not one-sided. For instance, how would you feel if you had a friend—let's call her Amelia—who only comes around when she wants to borrow something—like your fondue pot, your designer sunglasses, or your car with a full tank of gas? Amelia asks, "Could you babysit while I get the polish freshened on my toenails? Oh, and I need to unload big-time since my boss has become this miserly, manipulative, and mean-spirited mule of a man. Oh, and would you mind helping me with my daughter's costume for the school's talent show? This year she's a singing toad."

These might not be outrageous things to ask of a buddy, and yet if that's all Amelia ever came calling for, wouldn't you think your friend was a bit of a toad too? Why? Because you want a relationship in which someone not only needs you but loves you. Wouldn't you think that Amelia's brand of friendship wasn't intimate, wasn't real?

Christ would like to be our friend—a real one. And if we only go to Him in prayer, begging for a better job, better health, and a bigger house, might we not be sending the same message, that we're more interested in the "getting" than the loving?

Lord, please help me love You as a real friend and not just for what You can give me. Amen. —AH

6

ONE WORD THAT CHANGES EVERYTHING

He was despised and rejected by mankind,
a man of suffering, and familiar with pain.
Like one from whom people hide their faces he
was despised, and we held him in low esteem.
ISAIAH 53:3

Have you ever felt abandoned? Misplaced? Abused? Rejected? Forgotten? We have all felt those feelings from time to time. What can we do about them? Well, the world has plenty of answers. Mask the anguish with painkillers, addictions, false teachings under the guise of spiritual enlightenment, and myriad other bogus remedies. You name it, and the world is selling it as an alternative like the man hollering on the street corner selling snake oil. One soon discovers, though, that the world's answers are as real as the tooth fairy. Their cures will only make one feel more forlorn, emptier, and more forgotten than ever.

What to do? Face the unhappy pangs of this life by holding the hand of the one who has known all these trials—the one who knows better than anyone on earth what it feels like to suffer, to be rejected, abused, and forgotten. So, how does one do that, exactly? With the one word that the enemy of our souls wants us to forget. One word that can change everything—can bring meaning and hope and make that misery and aloneness flee to hell where it belongs.

It's prayer.

Father, help me to turn to You alone for my
comfort instead of the world. Amen. —AH

IMAGINE THIS. . .

*And all are justified freely by his grace through
the redemption that came by Christ Jesus.*
ROMANS 3:24

Imagine this. What if a stranger came up to you on the street and handed you a pearl necklace. Then after smiling, the man walked away? What would you do? Try to give the necklace back? Would you think it was stolen, or maybe that it was no more than a plastic bauble?

Yet what if you had it appraised and it was a genuine pearl necklace and valuable—in fact, a priceless treasure? You might then fret that the man would return and expect something from you—that you'd have to work to truly own such a costly gift. Or would you then think that the man was loony for offering such a precious gift to a mere stranger?

You get the drift. That is what Christ has done for us with His gift of life eternal—with His costly sacrifice on the cross. Still we treat Him like the man on the street, thinking He must be either phony or foolish, or that if He is real, there are strings attached to His good and perfect gift.

Okay, so what if we do finally understand this free gift of grace? What do we do with it? Accept it. Rejoice over it. Maybe even shout. Then thank Him—in that wonderful communication called prayer.

*Jesus, I want to be daily reminded of the pricelessness
of Your gift of grace. Thank You for all You
have done and continue to do. Amen. —AH*

THAT LITTLE
INNER MECHANISM

*"Do not let your hearts be troubled.
You believe in God; believe also in me."*
JOHN 14:1

There is something wonderful about a music box—that treasure chest of sweet and melodic tranquility—and if one believed in enchantment, it might be called the music of fairies. What if that music box were wound up over and over and over without ever letting it wind back down again? What if the little winding key got tighter and tighter until the inner mechanisms—like the cylinder, the comb, and the flywheel—could no longer work? It would no longer be able to play its beautiful music.

Well, when our hearts become troubled with the cares of this world, we can no longer play the music we were created to play. We are essentially broken. So, how does one undo, unravel, and slow down when our own winding key has been wound too tightly and our inner mechanism—our soul—can no longer function properly? We should take all our troubles to the Lord in prayer. Every heartache. Every disappointment. Every sorrow. He will let us rest in Him and disentangle ourselves from the human stresses so that we can rise again. So that we can once again play our music to a world that needs to hear it.

*Lord, when I am feeling anxious, help me to
remember that You hold me in the palm of
Your hand. You have the power to restore
and refresh my weary soul. Amen. —AH*

TUMBLING THE STONES

But just as he who called you is holy,
so be holy in all you do.
1 PETER 1:15

If you've ever spent time beachcombing, you know that the stones that get trapped in between the big rocks often get tossed and whirled a great deal. So much so that the edges get worked off, making them the smoothest of all. The colors and nuances and unique markings are accentuated. In other words, their beauty is brought out by the process of the constant stirring and abrasion—rock tumbling against rock. When you pick them up and roll them around in your palm, they feel like the shell of an egg. It's those stones that become part of your trove of little beach treasures.

God uses the tumbling turbulence of our lives to work off our edges—those jagged, sinful, rebellious edges that keep us from being all that we were meant to be.

Being tumbled can be painful—stone hitting stone can't be all that fun—but the outcome will be holiness and a loveliness of spirit. We will be treasures, brighter than diamonds and more precious than gold.

Pray that God can use your tumbling trials to bring out the beauty of your soul.

Dear Lord, please use the turbulent times
of my life to help make me beautiful in
my spirit, so that I can glorify You and be
all that You created me to be. —AH

WHEN OUR HEARTS ARE CAPTURED

Then you and the Levites and the foreigners residing among you shall rejoice in all the good things the LORD your God has given to you and your household.
DEUTERONOMY 26:11

How does a person react when standing at the mouth of the Grand Canyon—when he or she takes in the majestic spires and gorges that are awash in radiant color? What can a mother do when she holds her newborn baby for the first cuddling and cooing moments after birth—when the infant grasps her hand as if to say, "I know you!" How can we express delight when we stand under a fig tree, eating a piece of luscious fruit so ripe and juicy that it makes our taste buds do the tango? Or when our hearts are captured by a soul-aching melody or verse of poetry or the first glowing sparks of true love?

Our hearts long to thank someone, and it would only be natural to praise the giver of such gifts. Praise is prayer in one of its most beautiful forms. A grateful heart can more easily crowd out anger and envy, pride and strife. It can break open the most hardened heart to let in the light and splendor of heaven.

So, shall we raise our hands? Shall we create a hallelujah moment? Shall we rejoice in all the good things that the Lord your God has given us? We shall!

Father, thank You for all of the beauty, joy, and splendor that life has to offer. Please cultivate a grateful spirit in me. Amen. —AH

THE RADIANCE OF HIS SPLENDOR

In the year that King Uzziah died, I saw the Lord, high and exalted, seated on a throne; and the train of his robe filled the temple. Above him were seraphim, each with six wings: With two wings they covered their faces, with two they covered their feet, and with two they were flying.

ISAIAH 6:1–2

Society has used the words *awesome* and *incredible* and *glorious* so loosely for so long that the words no longer fill us with pause or wonder. Perhaps we mentally shrug when we hear those words batted about in conversation. People might say they had an incredible trip or they bought some awesome stilettos or they had a glorious day at the spa. In spite of this misapplication of these expressions, there are things that do fulfill the authentic meaning of these words.

The book of Isaiah tells us that the Lord is exalted, seated on a throne, and the train of His robe fills the temple. Isaiah also talks about the angels who attend Him and worship Him—that their wings cover their faces—surely because of the radiance of His splendor. How fearsome and humbling and magnificent that sight must be!

In fact, this holy scene in the heavenlies should remind us that one day every knee shall bow and every tongue confess that He is Lord. Why wait until that final day? Why not give praise to the one—the only one—who is worthy of our raised hearts and hands? The one who is truly incredible and awesome and glorious!

*Lord God, help me to comprehend
Your magnitude and glory. I want to be
awestruck by You. Amen. —AH*

THIS
COBBLESTONE JOURNEY

"I have told you these things, so that in me you may have peace. In this world you will have trouble. But take heart! I have overcome the world."
JOHN 16:33

When Americans travel to Europe, they will see that the streets of some of the more ancient cities are lined with charming paths of cobblestone. But the romance of these quaint streets and laneways stops cold when you trip and fall on the uneven stones. Yes, you will flail around. You will let out a shriek. Horror will flash across your face, but no one can reach you in time. You're on your own.

Then you hit the hard, unforgiving rock with brute force. There might be a bloody nose, a fractured cheekbone, a broken kneecap, as well as some painful scratches covering your palms. So, that merry strolling moment of joy has turned ugly. Suddenly that old-world look has as much charm as a French pastry lying in the dumpster.

Sounds a bit like life, doesn't it?

There is most excellent news, though. God's Word says that even though there will be trouble on life's path, He has overcome this world. Even when we tumble and cut ourselves on the sharp stones of life, it is comforting to know that He will not only mend our wounds in the here and now, but through the acceptance of His offer of redemption, He will someday take us away from this fallen world to a place that knows no pain, no trouble, no joy turned ugly. So, take heart, friends. He has overcome the world. Let's remember to thank Him daily!

Jesus, I have nothing to fear because You have prepared a way for me. I choose to trust in You. Amen. —AH

THE MOST
BEAUTIFUL WORDS

*So God created mankind in his own
image, in the image of God he created them;
male and female he created them.*
GENESIS 1:27

Flowers—bluebonnets, Mexican primrose, and Indian paintbrush—picked in delight on a spring day are sometimes pressed inside the pages of a book. When time passes, and one revisits the flowers, they are dried and flat and lifeless, mere shadows of what they were. The vibrant colors are gone, the perfume no longer enchants, and the wonder of their beauty is only a distant memory. Yet there lingers an endearing essence of what once was.

That is so much like humans in their fallen state.

We were made in the image of God, but because of sin, we became shriveled and faded. Yet with the sacrifice Jesus made for us with His very life, mankind has hope to return to the beauty that once was ours. When those who belong to Christ die and pass into eternity, they will be given glorified bodies renewed with life and color. Not for a short time like the flowers of the field, but for all eternity.

If you've never asked the Lord to be yours, to acknowledge your sin and take Him into your heart—well, what has been stopping you? They will be the most beautiful words you will ever speak and the most life-changing prayer you will ever pray.

*God, restore, refresh, and reconcile me
to Yourself. Help me to become all You
have created me to be. Amen. —AH*

AS EASY
AS BREATHING

Pray continually.
1 Thessalonians 5:17

Pray continually? Don't those two words in the Bible seem a bit foreign to us? In fact, the words stand alone—looking rather stark. We stare at them, wondering how anyone, no matter how holy, could accomplish such a command. There would be no time left for working or playing or eating or resting.

Perhaps the scripture means that to pray without ceasing is when we are in natural conversation with Him during the day—as if we were chatting with a friend on and off while taking a long pleasant walk together.

For instance, you might thank God when you wake up to a new morning. You might ask Him to bless your breakfast and invite Him to guide you through the day. You might feel compelled to breathe a prayer of thanksgiving when you have a near miss with another car on your way to work. Perhaps you'd want to praise Him for the project you successfully completed, and then request that He help your boss who's having a bad day or heal a coworker who's having some health issues. This kind of day does reflect the 1 Thessalonians scripture—that is, to stay so close to God that one finds praying as easy and comfortable as breathing.

*Father, please be present in my heart and
thoughts always. Never let our communion
and fellowship be severed. I want every area
of my life to be committed to You through
sincere, continual prayer. Amen. —AH*

SEEN
BY OTHERS

*"And when you pray, do not be like the hypocrites,
for they love to pray standing in the synagogues
and on the street corners to be seen by others.
Truly I tell you, they have received their reward in
full. But when you pray, go into your room, close
the door and pray to your Father, who is unseen."*

MATTHEW 6:5–6

Have you ever heard a beautiful prayer in a large cathedral, and the words echoed and sang with a stirring rhythm and spiritual uplift of its own? Some people are gifted at praying in public. They know how to move and excite their audiences with an eloquent presentation. Unfortunately, humans have to be careful not to enjoy the admiration of the crowd too much, since it would be easy to forget to whom the prayers are intended and begin to seek the approval of man over God.

Matthew encourages us to have a humble attitude when it comes to prayer by finding a quiet place to talk to Him, away from the attentive crowds. Does that mean we cannot pray in public? No, but it would be wise to be watchful of our motives, since a heartfelt closet prayer would surely be more welcome than a prayer that is raised up to impress the masses.

Where is your favorite quiet place to talk to God?

*Lord, give me a spirit of humility and sincerity when
I pray in front of others. Help me to remember
that prayer should not be used to show others
how godly and well-spoken I am but to connect
with You, the living God. Amen. —AH*

WHY FASTING?

"But when you fast, put oil on your head and wash your face, so that it will not be obvious to others that you are fasting, but only to your Father, who is unseen; and your Father, who sees what is done in secret, will reward you."
MATTHEW 6:17–18

Eating has become a sport in our country, a mania—perhaps even a god. So, to commit to giving up a meal or two occasionally or giving up solid food for a little while in order to spend more time with the Lord seems impossible.

It isn't.

What is the purpose of fasting? First of all, planning meals, buying food, cooking, and cleaning up is time-consuming, and when we give it up even for a day, it allows us more time to turn our hearts toward heaven. Secondly, fasting along with our prayer can be powerful as we hear the Lord more clearly, sense His presence more keenly, and see the work of the Holy Spirit moving in our lives. Fasting can give us a new perspective, one that is more God-centered, peace-filled, refreshing, freeing, healing, and life-changing.

If you have health issues that keep you from traditional fasting, you might try fasting TV shows or desserts. If you do fast and pray, the Gospel of Matthew says not to grandstand about it but to do it quietly, and then God will reward you.

Father, give me the desire and the discipline to seek You in prayer in a more devoted and focused way. Amen. —AH

ONE SOUL
AT A TIME

"If my people, who are called by my name, will humble
themselves and pray and seek my face and turn from
their wicked ways, then I will hear from heaven, and
I will forgive their sin and will heal their land."
2 CHRONICLES 7:14

If you have the courage to watch the evening news, you know that we live in perilous times. We also live in wicked times. People don't seem to care anymore about watching out for their neighbors. About lying and cheating a bit here and there. About living together first to see if that marriage thing might be for them. About honoring the sanctity of life and family and worship and God. In fact, the word *sin* has gone out of vogue, but just because a nation hides its transgressions doesn't mean they are getting away with them. Sound familiar? Just as Adam and Eve hid in the garden after they sinned, we as a nation are trying to hide our shame.

What can we do? It starts with one soul at a time. If we will humble ourselves and pray and seek His face and turn from our wicked ways, then He will hear us, forgive us, and heal our land. Let this be our personal petition, our greatest ambition, and our heart-prayer as a nation.

Lord, You have the power to guide and
restore nations. Please help the people
of this country to acknowledge their sin
and their need for You. Amen. —AH

A SACRAMENTAL OINTMENT

*Is anyone among you sick? Let them call the
elders of the church to pray over them and
anoint them with oil in the name of the Lord.*
JAMES 5:14

Sometimes when we think of the Bible, we think of such ancient people and cultures that the Holy Scriptures feel as close and accessible and understandable as a distant planet. Yet God has never changed. He is the same in our modern world as He was in ancient times. Even though the idea of an ill person being prayed over and anointed with oil by the elders of the church seems too archaic of a tradition to be considered today, think again.

In Bible times, people used oil for various reasons—both medicinal and spiritual. One purpose was to use oil like a sacramental ointment poured on someone's head as that person was prayed over for healing. There is, of course, no supernatural power in the oil itself, but God has the authority to use this act of obedience, this symbolic oil, as a way to heal.

So, when illness comes to you or your family in mind, body, or spirit, consider this scripture and know there is significance in the biblical traditions, even today.

*God, thank You for hearing my prayers—
whether they are quickly whispered or accompanied
with oil. Help me to better understand and
appreciate the traditions You have put in
place for Your followers. Amen. —AH*

THAT
VOLATILE LIQUID

"Therefore I tell you, do not worry about your life, what you will eat or drink; or about your body, what you will wear. Is not life more than food, and the body more than clothes? Look at the birds of the air; they do not sow or reap or store away in barns, and yet your heavenly Father feeds them. Are you not much more valuable than they?"
MATTHEW 6:25–26

Women tend to be like vats of worry. We toss everything imaginable into that emotional, messy brew. You know what I mean—the many frets that we distill when we choose to hand-wring through our days and toss and turn through our nights. Then we pour that volatile liquid into spray bottles, and we hose down our friends and family with it. Yeah, we're not talking about spritzing them with the calming and cooling lavender water that comes from a heart full of faith in the one who holds us in the palm of His mighty hand. We're talking about the muggy and malodorous perspiration from a life drenched in fear.

Jesus asks us if we can add a single hour to our life with worry. We cannot. Jesus also says that the birds are cared for and that we are much more valuable to Him. So, what are we to do?

We can pray.

It's real. It's powerful. And our friends and family will thank us!

Father, remind me that You're in control.
I place my burdens and fears in Your
capable hands. Amen. —AH

ALMOST TOO MUCH TO HOPE FOR

Husbands, love your wives, just as Christ loved the church and gave himself up for her.
EPHESIANS 5:25

Everybody loves a wedding. Why? Well, beyond the scrumptious food, the enchanting attire, and the glorious setting—the idea of a man and woman, speaking words of tender affection, so deeply in love and so attentive to each other's joy and delight, it's contagious, intoxicating, and unabashedly beautiful.

To think that is the way Christ loves us is almost too much to take in. It is almost too much to hope for.

Yet it is the truth.

Christ loves us intimately and passionately, not romantically as in human terms, but with a steadfast care and devotion that is beyond our human understanding. His love is forever. Imagine the God of the universe with such perfect love. For you. For me. Who can resist that kind of sweet affection? Who among you really wants to turn your back on this exquisite overture of love? It is contagious, intoxicating, and unabashedly beautiful!

So then, reach your heart to heaven.

Embrace His love.

The Lord is waiting for your prayerful answer, and He is hoping it will be yes!

God, the depth of Your love is unfathomable. I want to be swept up in it and transformed by it. Amen. —AH

WHERE WE BELONG

*Jesus, knowing that they intended to
come and make him king by force,
withdrew again to a mountain by himself.*
JOHN 6:15

When Jesus came, people saw Him in a hundred different ways, and what they wanted from Him wasn't always salvation. They sought political power. They wanted freedom, not always from their fallen state, but from their enemies. They wanted a king who could be their champion, their leader, their conqueror for all their causes.

But Jesus? Well, He was much more concerned about their hearts and prayers than the power He could wield. Jesus didn't come to overthrow empires but to overthrow sin and death. Not to fight against political enemies but to fight against the enemy (Satan) of our souls.

Jesus is a king, yes. In fact, He is the King of kings and Lord of lords. He will indeed reign forever and ever. While on earth, He said, "Follow Me." He was the Good Shepherd, and He came with a staff, not a sword. He wanted to lead us not into a worldly battle but away from hell. Away from all that is unholy and toward the home where we belong.

So, when Christ says, "Follow Me," what do you do? Where is your heart? What is your prayer?

*Jesus, help me to follow You with boldness, joy,
and trust. I want to see life through heaven-
bound eyes. Be my everything. Amen. —AH*

A DAILY JOLT
FOR THE SPIRIT

*In all your ways submit to him,
and he will make your paths straight.*
PROVERBS 3:6

Have you ever been caught in a rut for so long that it started to feel like a hopeless abyss? That is just where the enemy of your soul wants you to be—unable to be effective in this hurting and needy world, unable to share the love of Christ, unable to reflect His glorious light.

So, how does one emerge from those endless furrows that represent the monotone, monochrome grind of the everyday—the looking down into the mire instead of gazing up into the splendor? Just like the vehicle stuck in the rut, sometimes we need a jolt to pull us out. Prayer is that daily jolt for our spirit. Prayer is what gets us back on track, headed where we need to go.

If we submit to God in prayer, He will guide us on this earthly road. He will help us stay out of that dreaded rut and free of the daily abyss of hopelessness, so that we might rise up and be all that Christ wants us to be in a world that needs His love.

That is a promise we can take to our knees every day.

*Holy Spirit, don't ever let me lose hope. You
are my protector, provider, and comforter.
Even when I feel desperately alone and
downtrodden, help me to remember that You
are always there for me. Amen. —AH*

WHEN LIFE
HANDS YOU LEMONS

*And we know that in all things God works for
the good of those who love him, who have
been called according to his purpose.*
ROMANS 8:28

Your boss recommends a new hire for a promotion—the same position you'd been working toward for ten years. Your best friend betrays your trust in a way that makes you question all your relationships. A long-needed and much-anticipated vacation must be canceled because of illness. What is this?

It's called life.

You've heard the old saying that one should make lemonade out of the lemons that life hands you, and yet you wonder, *Where is the sugar? The chipped ice? The crystal pitcher to put it all in?*

And then you realize that the world expects you to provide all the extras with your own personal ingenuity and grit. Yet the steam that comes from our own strength will soon run out. We humans weren't meant to go it alone. We were meant for a relationship with God. Through Christ, that sweet connection is restored. He is the one who will help us. He promises us that if we love Him, He will work all things for good. He will redeem all things. He alone has the power to make the sweetest lemonade out of the sourest of lemons.

What a promise. What a prayer!

*Father, thank You for taking what is miserable
and tragic and working it for good through
Your power and sovereignty. Help me to
trust in Your promises. Amen. —AH*

HURTERS
OR HEALERS?

*"A new command I give you: Love one another.
As I have loved you, so you must love one
another. By this everyone will know that you
are my disciples, if you love one another."*
JOHN 13:34–35

We have a choice each morning as we wake up to a new day. Will we be the kind of person who causes more hurt in the world, or will we be healers? Will we be a battering blow to someone's spirit instead of a blessing? Will we choose love when it's easier to hate? This choice is ours with every word we speak. Every action we take. Every thought that passes through our minds. For everything has an effect.

Everything.

The Lord's command is to love one another. How hard can that be? Pretty hard when it comes to loving the unlovable. To be honest, loving prickly people—not you and me, of course—well, it's as easy as giving a porcupine a big bear hug. Not pleasant.

But God can make possible what appears impossible to man. Through prayer, the Lord can help us love those who appear unlovable.

So what will you choose to be when you get up in the morning to a new dawn—a hurter or a healer? The world has an overabundant supply of the former and a serious shortage of the latter!

*God, give me the strength and patience to encounter
the world with the abounding love of Christ.
Help me to love as You love. Amen. —AH*

25

HEAVIER THAN
I CAN CARRY

"For my yoke is easy and my burden is light."
MATTHEW 11:30

Kids are so honest. Don't you love their direct, unguarded approach to life? It's refreshing to see, since as we grow up we tend to become more closed off and less open and vulnerable with other people, with God, and with ourselves.

For instance, if a child is walking alongside her dad at the beach, and she is trying to carry a full bucket of wet sand, most likely she will turn to her father easily, happily, and expectantly to say, "Daddy, can you carry this? It's too heavy for me."

That is how our Father in heaven would like us to come to Him in prayer. We weren't created to carry the heavy burdens of this world. We were made for better things, for loftier things—for joy and peace and love and laughter. For harmony.

So, when we are burdened in this life, let us take on the guileless honesty of a child. Let us turn to Him and, like the little girl, say to God, "Daddy, this is too heavy. Can You carry this for me?" Then we can let it go, whatever it is, into His hands—easily, happily, and expectantly.

Father, please take away my heavy burdens.
Just as a child trusts her earthly father, help
me to trust You with every aspect of my
life. I give it all to You. Amen. —AH

GOT PRAYER?

The LORD is near to all who call on him,
to all who call on him in truth.
PSALM 145:18

Prayer is communicating with God. Wow, really? You mean, we can connect with the Creator of the universe like He's our best friend, only better? Yes, that's it. Sounds unbelievable and more than a little audacious, doesn't it? Yet it's what God desires of us. A sweet and holy rapport. A relationship. Communion.

Still hard to grasp? Perhaps the concept seems so inconceivably wonderful and so simplistic that man feels a need to add to the process, give it his own style, and do it his own way. Perhaps even conjure up his own gods. Yet man cannot change what God has ordained. It would be like filling our car's gas tank with a fuel mixture from miscellaneous liquids we found in the garage, which would, of course, ruin the car for any good use.

Maybe it's easier to explain what biblical prayer is not: Prayer is not meditation. Prayer is not happy thoughts or wishful thinking. Prayer is not sitting in a certain position and clearing one's mind. Prayer is not chanting, visualization, or communicating with a spirit guide.

Prayer is talking directly to God, through Jesus Christ. It is indeed that simple. That intimate. That inconceivably wonderful!

Got prayer?

Creator God, help me to grasp the beautiful simplicity
of prayer. I want an unceasing, rich communion
with You, my Lord and Savior. Amen. —AH

THE
PRISONER'S PRAYER

If you declare with your mouth, "Jesus is Lord," and believe in your heart that God raised him from the dead, you will be saved. For it is with your heart that you believe and are justified, and it is with your mouth that you profess your faith and are saved.
ROMANS 10:9–10

We are all prisoners on death row. Yet Christ, with His sacrifice on the cross, has thrown open the cell door for us. All we need to do is walk through. Take His hand as He walks us through the iron gates, the tower with armed guards, the concrete barriers, the barbed wire, and out into the beautiful blue sky of redemption.

Why do some people insist on staying in the confines of a prison cell when beyond the walls of sin is freedom? It comes down to one tormenting word. . .*pride*.

Pride keeps us paralyzed; it keeps us fooling ourselves. Pride allows us to accept the lies of Satan: that we are better off on our own, calling our own shots. How else can we convince ourselves that a dark and cold dungeon is better than the pure, warm light that streams through the window?

Once again, Christ has already broken our chains. He's opened the prison door. All we need to do is walk through.

The prisoner's prayer of freedom is on our lips. It is written in our hearts by the Holy Spirit. Will we stay or step out into the warm rays of redemption?

Heavenly Father, I believe that Jesus died for my sins and that He is Lord. Please forgive my rebellion and come into my heart. Amen. —AH

THE VOICE
OF HEAVEN

*Jesus answered, "I am the way and
the truth and the life. No one comes to
the Father except through me."*
JOHN 14:6

The world says, "What can you give me?" God wants us to say, "How may I help you?" The world says, "I need more." God would like us to say, "I am content. Let me share what I have." The world says, "I can make it on my own. I can save myself." God would like us to say, "Lord, You made me. You're the way, the truth, and the life. Let's walk this dusty road together."

The world never seems to be in sync with what God wants for us, dreams for us. We get the idea that what the fallen earth has to offer is more fascinating and glorious and irresistible. Yet how can that be, when people fail us and everything that *can* fall apart *does* fall apart? When even the kings and queens of this earth are destined to the same lonely and hopeless end without divine assistance?

There are no answers in this earthy dust, only in the voice of heaven. We should look up to our hope—for it lies in Christ and Christ alone. He is life, not death. He is the most fascinating and glorious and irresistible hope there ever was or ever will be. This could be our heart-praise as dawn arrives and as the sun sets.

*God, You are the answer to the riddles
and the problems of life. You are the salve
for my sin-sick soul. Amen. —AH*

DO YOU BELIEVE
IN MIRACLES?

Now while he was in Jerusalem at the
Passover Festival, many people saw the signs he
was performing and believed in his name.
JOHN 2:23

Jesus asks us to believe in miracles. Do you believe?

Sometimes when we pray, we go away, believing nothing will happen. Maybe our heart-prayer should be as the boy's father in the Bible who exclaimed, "Lord, I believe. Help my unbelief!"

God does answer every prayer. It just may not fit our agenda. The answer might come as a yes, a no, or a wait. When miracles do come, it is easy to forget as the Israelites did, even though they witnessed miracle after miracle after miracle. Still, they doubted.

That is the nature of man.

So, let us keep a prayer journal and write down the answers to our prayers, the miracles we experience. They do happen. The journal will be a reminder that God is listening. That God does care about our comings and goings. That He is still all-powerful and able to perform signs and wonders. When the miracles do come, write them down. Praise Him for them. Tell others. From time to time, we should go back and read the journal, see the long list of His tender mercies, so that we might be encouraged.

What miracle are you praying for today?

Lord, don't let me forget the countless prayers
You have answered. Don't let me doubt
the power of prayer. Amen. —AH

TOO EASY

*Isaac prayed to the LORD on behalf
of his wife, because she was childless.*
GENESIS 25:21

I know several families right now who are making the same request Isaac made. "God, please, please give us a child." It's the kind of prayer that can be prayed for weeks, months, and years on end, or the kind that comes all at once, rushing in like some desperate wind.

For Isaac, it all seemed so simple. He prayed. God answered. His wife became pregnant with not just one baby but two! So what are we to tell all the people who are still waiting for their answer? What are we to tell the ones who never get a baby of their own? Have they just not tried hard enough? Perhaps they didn't say the right words, or maybe God just doesn't think they would be fit parents.

Or maybe it's just not that easy. Some people pray and seem to get the answers they wanted. Others seem to get handed a harder pill to swallow. I don't think we can know all the plans God has for us.

What we can know is that God is in control, that He hears us, and that He loves us. And the best thing we can do for someone praying for a child is not to try to come up with some explanation for why their prayer hasn't been answered. The best thing is just to keep praying with them.

*Lord, help me to remember that Your answers
aren't always easy ones. Amen.* —ML

THUNDERSTORMS

Ask the Lord for rain in the springtime;
it is the Lord who sends the thunderstorms.
ZECHARIAH 10:1

I'm afraid when it comes to rain, we can all be fair-weather friends. Many people love a gentle, warm sprinkle. But cold, spitting droplets on a November day is enough to give a person a migraine.

In the dry, hot days of summer, everyone is likely to plead with God for rain. Farmers need it for their crops. Children want to play in it and be refreshed. Gardens are crying out for help with their wilting leaves.

But the rain most of us have in mind is probably something along the lines of a quiet, steady shower. We don't necessarily want the driving, violent thunderstorm.

The God who opens the heavens to give flowers a drink is also the God who sends crashing thunder and streaks of lightning. It is good to be reminded of that.

Our God is gentle and warm. Our God is big and powerful. Praise Him for all He is.

Lord, thank You for speaking to me in gentle
whispers and in strong proclamations. Please
help me to honor You always. Amen. —ML

BIG EARS

Evening, morning and noon I cry
out in distress, and he hears my voice.
PSALM 55:17

A child once was asked to draw a picture of God. She drew an old man with a long white beard, striking blue eyes, and humongous ears. When asked why God's ears were so large, the girl replied, "God listens to everyone all the time around the whole world. That takes big ears!"

Aren't you glad God has big ears? That He is able to listen to us all the time, no matter where we go or what time of day it is?

David wrote in Psalm 55 of a time of tremendous personal stress. "I am distraught" and "My heart is in anguish within me," he said (vv. 2 and 4). Why was he in such trouble? He reveals the answer in verses 12–13: "If an enemy were insulting me, I could endure it. . . . But it is you, a man like myself, my companion, my close friend."

Betrayed! Is there any kind of trouble that causes more worry and heartache? Betrayal gnaws at us day and night—there is no end to the wondering why and the self-doubt.

Thank goodness God has big ears. We can take our heaviest burdens to Him and He will hear us. Only He can silence the voices of doubt and despair in our heads.

"As for me, I call to God, and the LORD saves me" (Psalm 55:16). Yes, David. Us too.

Lord, thank You for Your big ears! Amen. —ML

IN ALL CIRCUMSTANCES

*Rejoice always, pray continually,
give thanks in all circumstances; for this
is God's will for you in Christ Jesus.*
1 Thessalonians 5:16–18

To-Do List: Go to store, pay bills, see about plumber, take kids to practice, pick up kids from practice, dentist, cancel appointment, text friend, pray, make dinner, put laundry in washer, walk dog, go to bed.

Is prayer even on your to-do list? More often than not, we forget to set aside specific time for prayer. Perhaps it gets put off until there's quiet in the house, until we are not so tired, until our work is done, until. . .

It is good to remember that we don't even have to set aside a certain special time. We don't have to sit in a prayer chair or wear a prayer robe. Our God is always there for us. We can talk to Him anytime. Indeed, we should.

Let's go back to that to-do list—how might your day go with prayer as your inner soundtrack? *God, thank You that I have so many choices of foods to eat. Help me feed those who are hungry. Thank You for the income we have. Thank You for the skills and talents of others. Thank You for healthy kids. . .*and on and on and on.

It's good to have special times set aside for rest and reflection. But it's also good to remember you don't have to wait until then.

*Lord, thank You for always being
there for me. Amen.* —ML

ALL OF
THE ABOVE

*For the LORD gives wisdom; from his
mouth come knowledge and understanding.*
PROVERBS 2:6

Every day is full of so many decisions—from the time we wake up till the time our eyelids drop heavily at night, we are faced with decisions both small and significant. *What should I wear? What should I have for breakfast? What am I going to do today? What am I doing with my life?* It's easy to get overwhelmed, even before your cereal has a chance to get soggy.

It's also easy to fall into the trap of thinking that if we simply pray about an issue, God will give us the answer—and in fairly short order. Because God knows we need all the answers we need when we need them, and not a moment later. Right?

It seems that often when we want an answer, the only thing that will do is the answer we want. Nothing less. Yet God, our generous Father, has something better in mind. We want a solution; He wants to give us the formula. We want a simple yes or no; He wants to give us time to see if we even asked the right question. We want A, B, C, or D; He wants to give us all of the above.

*Thank You, Lord, that Your ways are higher
and wiser and better than mine. Help me to be
patient when I lack wisdom and to see Your
knowledge and understanding. Amen. —ML*

PRAYER OF COMPLAINT

*"What have I done to displease you that
you put the burden of all these people on me?"*
NUMBERS 11:11

Have you ever felt the weight of the responsibility of guiding, teaching, leading, and encouraging others? This point in Moses' story is just one of many when he became frustrated with those complaining Israelites. He must have longed for his days as a shepherd, when he could just give the animals a poke or two with his staff to get them to go in the right direction. This Israelite flock was a different story—disobedient, fickle, petty, and selfish. Basically, a normal group of human beings.

Moses knew what to do. He did what he often did when feeling overwhelmed—he talked to God. No, his prayer wasn't pretty—it wasn't full of praise and honor. One might say he was even a little snarky—"Did I conceive all these people? Did I give them birth?" (v. 12).

Chances are, you've voiced your own prayer of complaint a time or two. And you know what? God didn't crush you. God knows our hearts. He knew Moses' heart. Before Moses even began his rant, God saw his need and heard his plea. So the Lord gave Moses the answer he needed—friends. "They will share the burden of the people with you so that you will not have to carry it alone" (v. 17).

*Lord, help me remember to call on You
first when I'm feeling overwhelmed. Thank
You for being my friend. Amen. —ML*

ACCEPTED

*The Lord has heard my cry for
mercy; the Lord accepts my prayer.*
PSALM 6:9

The machine quietly whirs. It eats the paper, slurping it up like a mechanical frog pulling in a fly on its tongue. You wait. And wait. Some ticking and chinking and clunking are heard. Then the wrinkled slip of faded green comes rolling out again.

Denied.

What is it about those money-taking devices on vending machines and at the self-pay cash registers that so easily angers a person? Maybe it's the feeling of rejection. You willingly submit your hard-earned cash as a trade for a parking ticket, or a can of soda pop, or, yes, a large hunk of brightly wrapped chocolate that you really, really need. Right now.

But no. No joy. No simple acceptance of the offering. No chocolate.

Thanks be to God for accepting what you give Him. Even when your prayers are feeble or not well spoken. Even when perhaps all you can do is cry. Even when low blood sugar is talking and you blurt out angry words. God hears you and accepts your prayer.

The machine quietly whirs. The paper once more gets eaten by the mechanical mouth. But this time, it disappears for good. A satisfying clunk is heard as the desired object is dropped down, and then you receive it.

Accepted.

*Thank You, Lord, for accepting my prayer,
even when I don't exactly know what to say.
Thank You for listening to me. Amen.* —ML

THE
BEGGAR KING

"Hear the supplication of your servant."
1 Kings 8:30

Solomon was a wise king. He had all the power of Israel in his hands. He built a magnificent temple, which he was chosen by God to build. He decided hard cases for his people and had riches that were the envy of the world.

Yet in his prayer to God, he sounded like a beggar.

Supplication is not a word that gets used much these days. It comes from a Latin root that means to plead humbly or beg. It's not the kind of action you would expect from a powerful monarch. Yet the Bible is full of unlikely people doing unexpected things.

Over and over in his prayer, Solomon humbled himself and asked for God to hear, to act, and to forgive. He didn't place himself above God or ask for things he didn't need. He didn't highlight his own achievements or the greatness of his people. Rather, he focused heavily on their potential downfalls and their sin.

Standing before the "vast assembly" of Israel (v. 65), he showed his people exactly who was in charge, who was taking care of them, and who they should count on. Not him. Not Solomon the king. But the Lord, the God of Israel. For "the LORD is God and. . .there is no other" (v. 60).

God, there is no one like You. Help me to show others that anything good in my life comes from You, and nowhere else. Amen. —ML

LESS
IS MORE

*"They devour widows' houses and
for a show make lengthy prayers."*
MARK 12:40

When did quantity start being valued over quality? It probably goes back to ancient times. One guy starts collecting rocks. Another guy makes a bigger pile of rocks. And on it goes.

Greed is what makes people keep grabbing for more. That feeling of wanting what you cannot really ever hope to get on your own. The feeling of being powerless and needing something—and lots of it—to fill the void.

The teachers of the law were afflicted with this disease. They had a measure of respect and power, but they wanted more. It was not enough for some of the people to acknowledge their greatness—they wanted everyone to do so. They must have known that the real power and honor and wisdom was nothing they could claim.

So they wore long robes, and took long strides, and sat at long tables, and voiced long prayers—all to show that they deserved respect.

Just after Jesus comments about these teachers devouring widows' houses, we see Jesus sitting down, watching the crowds bringing their offerings. From the hands of the rich and powerful came large, showy quantities of coins. But a poor widow gave only a couple of pennies.

"Truly I tell you," Jesus said, "this poor widow has put more into the treasury than all the others" (v. 43). The lesson was clear.

*Lord, please make me humble. Help me
to use my words and actions to point to
You, instead of myself. Amen.* —ML

COMFORTABLE

*Praise be to the God and Father of our Lord
Jesus Christ, the Father of compassion and the God
of all comfort, who comforts us in all our troubles,
so that we can comfort those in any trouble.*
2 Corinthians 1:3–4

A goose feather–filled duvet. The purring cat curled up by the crackling fire. The aroma of chocolate chip cookies baking in the oven. Soft rain on a cloudy day, a good book, and a cup of tea.

Everyone has their favorite sources of comfort. When a work day hasn't gone well, a rather large bill has arrived, a fight has occurred, or a loved one is suffering, people reach out for a security blanket—in the form of a person, place, or thing.

Humans need that tangible reminder of safety, peace, and strength. It starts from the moment those little bodies burst out of the womb and into the foreign air. The cries go up, the hands reach out, and the tiny fingers grasp for anyone who will bundle them up and make them feel they are not alone.

God loves us so much; He feels our worries and bears our troubles, and He reaches out to us through His words and His songs and His reminders of love that come in all the little ways He knows will suit us best. He comforts us through the hands and feet of others who embrace us in hard times.

*Lord, help me to be a comfort to others in
the ways You comfort me. Amen.* —ML

LIES

If a ruler listens to lies,
all his officials become wicked.
PROVERBS 29:12

"Oh, be careful little ears what you hear." Have you heard that song? It was taught to little children in churches many years ago. The song is about protecting your heart by monitoring what goes into your ears and eyes and so on. Generally when someone talks about protecting your ears, they are talking about things such as bad language, or dirty jokes, or, perhaps, wrong-headed theology. Yet many people, whether rulers or not, would do well to heed this proverb.

This proverb paints an interesting story in just one line. Imagine the once-respected, once-popular ruler, perhaps weighed down with daily decisions, seeks advice from someone. Someone she trusts, but who has not earned her trust. Someone wise by worldly standards, someone who knows how to please. This someone spins tales in her ear, stories of triumphs and treasure, of winning respect and arguments and. . .votes.

Once the ruler listens to the lies, her officials see that lying is the way to be heard. You see, they don't start out wicked. They "become" wicked—because they realize that is the way to get attention, to gain power, to find a listening ear.

Yet what would have happened if the ruler had been listening to truth instead? What would have happened if the ruler had spent more time listening to God in prayer?

Dear Lord, help me to remember to listen
to You and not just talk. Amen. —ML

GROCERY
PRAYER LIST

*For from him and through him and for him are
all things. To him be the glory forever! Amen.*
ROMANS 11:36

God, thank You for the produce: for bananas and grapes, and carrots and cucumbers. Thank You even for brussels sprouts and for the lowly potato. Thank You for an abundance of crops and healthy foods. Thank You for the men and women who farm the land and take care of the orchards, for the ones who pilot the boats and planes and tractors and trains, for all the people involved in harvesting this food, so shoppers can buy a fresh pineapple to enjoy.

God, thank You for the people who care for the livestock that produce the meat we eat and for the fishers who gather the bounty from the sea. Thank You for many hours of hard work that go into producing all the ingredients so cooks can create the perfect meat loaf.

Thank You for milk that nourishes little bones and teeth and helps everyone grow. Thank You for all the milk substitutes and that for every dietary need these days there is, somewhere, a product that will satisfy.

Thank You for the household goods in plentiful supply. Especially for toilet paper, Lord. Thank You for toilet paper. Enough said.

And thank You for convenience foods that make life a little easier, for doesn't everyone once in a while need to make dinner in just one minute and fifteen seconds?

For all these things, Lord, we thank You. Amen. —ML

BODY TALK

If the whole body were an ear,
where would the sense of smell be?
1 CORINTHIANS 12:17

One big ear. Can you imagine it? If everybody walking around your neighborhood today did not have hands and feet and noses and bellies, but just one big ear? It seems like some kind of bizarre nightmare. Body piercings would be even more prevalent. Wax removal would be big business. And just imagine the size of the Q-tips!

Thanks be to God that we are not all giant ears, but that instead people have many parts. And indeed, that as one body in Christ, there are many different kinds of people, with many different kinds of gifts and abilities.

At times it seems life would be a lot easier if everyone could think and talk and walk alike. But if you've ever been a part of a team of people working toward a common goal, you know how valuable it is to have members of the team be able to contribute in different ways to the different aspects of the work.

So if today you are annoyed by someone, perhaps someone who is quite different from you, try to imagine what life would be like if everyone was the same. Then be thankful for the differences you encounter—even the annoying ones. Just think, it could be a lot worse. You could be shopping for giant Q-tips!

Lord, thank You for Your amazing creative
powers. Help me to appreciate every person
as a part of Your creation. Amen. —ML

IT TAKES
AN ARMY

*David went down with his men to fight against
the Philistines, and he became exhausted.*
2 Samuel 21:15

In 2 Samuel 21, David is king—not the shepherd who killed Goliath and frightened away the Philistine army with a single stone. He is an older man and cannot endure the rigors of battle.

Isn't it comforting to know even King David became exhausted? Sure, he was fighting a battle against powerful warriors and not just doing laundry. But stain fighting is hard work too, right?

Once again, a heavily armed and vengeful Philistine threatened David's life. One of David's men killed the warrior. Then David's men decided their king's life would not be endangered again. "Never again will you go out with us to battle, so that the lamp of Israel will not be extinguished" (v. 17).

In biblical context, kings could make any laws they wanted and rule as they saw fit. But a king without an army is a sitting target. Without an army to support and protect him, David would have died on the battlefield that day.

Have you thanked God today for the army of supporters that allow you to accomplish your work? Have you thanked the friends and family members who look out for you, protect you, and give you a chance to rest? If you haven't, go ahead. Put down this book and do it now.

*Thank You, God, for all the people who
help me survive every day. Amen. —ML*

A WARNING

Do not be arrogant, but tremble.
ROMANS 11:20

In Romans 11, Paul delivers this rather stark warning. He has been talking about the Israelites, and how they did not receive all the blessings they could have received because of their disobedience. He reminds the Gentiles to not feel as though they are superior simply because they have been granted salvation—a place of standing in the family of God. No, instead he encourages them to remember that they are just a branch of a very old and long-standing tree. Just as God has pruned the tree before, they are vulnerable to trimming as well. It is only through faith, which comes from God, that any people can belong to the Creator of all.

Can you think of any people today who act as though they own the market when it comes to true Christianity? That they are the real Christians and others are just lame imitations? If you've lived long enough, you will know that just about every person who ever called on the name of the Lord has at one time or another made the mistake of thinking they were the only ones who knew how to pronounce that name just right.

Tremble at the almighty power of our great God, who gives, and takes away, and gives again out of His abundant grace. Let us strive to be so generous.

*Dear Lord, help me be more filled with faith
than I am with criticism. Amen.* —ML

AWARD-WINNING LAZINESS

A sluggard buries his hand in the dish;
he is too lazy to bring it back to his mouth.
PROVERBS 26:15

Wow. Did a picture just form in your head? A picture of the person who would win the Laziest Person Ever Award (though of course, they'd be too lazy to come and claim it)?

It's a beautiful description. You can just see the person. Sitting there at a table laden with goodies, his rolls of fat piling up over his belt. He reaches a swollen hand into a casserole, grabbing a piece that would feed a family of five. He sighs heavily, as if even exhaling takes an effort. His arm hangs limply, balanced on the edge of the table. What will he do? Will he eat the casserole? Will he keel over from cholesterol overload?

Before your mind goes on painting this lovely picture, you might want to do a personal faith-check.

God has given you tremendous blessings—a world full of gifts to enjoy, good work to do, family and friends to love, and a grace that knows no bounds. Yet how many of us sit there at His table with our hands just lying in the plenty, refusing to do the work of faith required to receive what God has in store? Avoiding reading His Word, forgetting to pray, pretending that faith is not a discipline but just another dish on the table.

Lord, help me not to be lazy in my
pursuit of You. Amen. —ML

PREPARATIONS

Always be prepared to give an answer
to everyone who asks you to give the
reason for the hope that you have.
1 PETER 3:15

Painting is like many manual jobs in that a good deal of the work involved in this task happens in the preparations. Selecting the paint, buying the paint, buying the tools, clearing out the furniture, cleaning the surfaces, taping up the areas not to be painted, laying down the drop cloths, priming the surfaces, letting them dry, stirring the paint, setting up a ladder, and pouring the paint. Finally, after all of that (and no doubt you expert painters out there will note any steps left out), you paint.

The same is true for telling others about your faith in Christ. People often feel nervous or reluctant to talk to people about their faith, and it seems likely that part of that is to do with a lack of preparation. If you practice your faith daily by talking with God, studying His Word, talking with other believers about questions you have, and serving others, you will feel more confident about describing what your faith is all about. It will be easier to give the reason for the hope that you have if you are actually living in that hope every day. Why not begin your preparations right now?

Dear Lord, thank You for the hope we have
through Jesus Christ, Your Son. Amen. —ML

SEEKER FRIENDLY

"If you seek him, he will be found by you."
1 Chronicles 28:9

Somewhere in the '90s, the seeker-friendly trend began to grow among Christian churches. The idea was to craft worship services that were not exclusionary but welcoming and appealing to masses of people who either did not know God at all or just were not regular churchgoers. This trend manifested itself in different ways, depending on the church. For some people, seeker-friendly meant incorporating secular pop music or film clips into the service. For others, seeker-friendly meant just opening the church doors.

Whatever way it showed up, the idea was people needed help to seek God. They couldn't find Him on their own. Now, there is too little space here on this page to argue the ins and outs of or whys and hows and reasons seeker-friendly services are or are not good ideas. But one thing seems pretty clear from scripture:

God is seeker friendly. He is not hiding from you. He is not turning His back on you. He is not a bouncer at the gate, judging you based on what jeans you are wearing or how many tattoos you have. He welcomes all who are seeking to find Him. The details will get sorted out later.

Lord, help me to seek You every day. Amen. —ML

A CONVERSATION

"Simon son of John, do you love me more than these?"
JOHN 21:15

There's a beautiful recording of an example of prayer in John 21. It's a conversation that took place between Peter and Jesus, after Jesus had risen from the dead and had appeared to His disciples. Three times in the conversation Jesus asks Peter about his love for Him, and three times He gives Peter a command to take care of or feed His sheep.

People often have similar conversations with God in prayer. God asks something of you, and you respond. He asks again, and you respond again. He asks again, and so on. If you're honest, you'll admit that there's probably a good reason you keep hearing the same question asked of you again and again.

Let's face it—Simon Peter isn't exactly pictured as the tender-loving type in the Bible accounts that include him. He's more of a go-getter, a doer of the Word, not a lover of the people. So it's not surprising to hear Jesus pressing him on the subject that was likely to be a point of weakness for him.

So what is Jesus pressing you about? What question have you heard God asking you over and over again? What has your response been? Better yet, what will it be?

Dear Father in heaven, thank You for our
conversations. Help me to constantly listen for
what You have to say to me. Amen. —ML

CALL TO ACTION

"We must obey God rather than human beings!"
ACTS 5:29

The struggle for obedience is as old as the idea of chore lists. Whenever humans are faced with a requirement, we have a natural bent toward disobedience.

Here Peter shouts out a call to action through the centuries. "We must obey God rather than human beings!"

Now, any teenagers who happen to read this should take note. Peter does not say we should *dis*obey human beings—particularly your parents.

It's just that when it comes to following the orders of men and women or following God, the choice should be a no-brainer, right? Let's not kid ourselves. The choice isn't always that easy to figure out. Sometimes people might even find themselves following someone who claims to be speaking the Word of God, only to discover the person was really speaking lies.

When Peter shouted this out, he was facing a very real possibility of being put to death for proclaiming Christ. Odds are, not many now reading this book will face such an extreme situation as Peter's. Yet it should encourage us to keep stepping forward. If Peter can face death and still obey, people today should be able to face discomfort and do likewise.

One last thing to note about Peter's call—he didn't shout alone; the apostles were replying together with him. You're not alone either.

Dear Father God, help me to obey You
every step of the way. Amen. —ML

COMMANDING PRESENCE

Trouble and distress have come upon me,
but your commands give me delight.
PSALM 119:143

Not often does a person in trouble look up from their sobbing and cry, "Please, somebody, give me some commands!"

The word *commands* is not generally seen in a positive light. Commanding someone sounds too authoritative, too bossy, and too pushy. People don't want to be commanded—they'd rather be guided, led, or called.

Yet God commands. When people come into His commanding presence in prayer, they do find comfort. Why? Because when the foundations of your life are shaken, you want to hold on to something that is real, that is true, that will not and cannot be moved. The law of the Lord is that. Moreover, His law is *good*.

The more you meditate on His Word, the more you'll be convinced of this. God's laws for living together and loving one another are evidence of a mind high above ours—a mind not hampered by a constant focus on self. Use the laws of God in your prayer time, and you will be forced to think about others, to consider what it means to really live in community, and to put others before yourself. In that process, the sorrow and trouble that is weighing you down will not disappear, but will be put in proper perspective and, thus, become a little bit of a lighter load.

Lord, thank You for the comfort You
bring us in Your law. Amen. —ML

WITHOUT PUNISHMENT

The punishment that brought us peace was on him, and by his wounds we are healed.
ISAIAH 53:5

If you are a caregiver to children, you have witnessed the relief that punishment can bring. A child does a bad thing. That child tries to cover up aforementioned bad thing. The child becomes increasingly miserable and/or mired in more trouble as the deceit rises to ridiculous proportions. Finally the child is punished, and after the required amount of sobbing, yelling, or complaining has been achieved, the child goes and plays in peace. All is right with the world. . .for now.

In each of us is a built-in, God-created desire for justice. We want good to win over evil. We want wrongs to be made right. We want no bad guy to go free. Even, as it turns out, if that bad guy happens to be us.

When we pray and ask for peace, it would be good to remember we are asking the one who created peace—the only one through whom our peace can ultimately come. Only Jesus can give us that. It is by His wounds we are healed, no one else's. His wounds are our punishment—a punishment we would not have been able to bear. God loves us so; He wanted us to be able not just to survive but to live eternally.

Dear Jesus, thank You for taking on what we could not. Please help us to live to understand Your peace. Amen. —ML

BE QUIET

"In repentance and rest is your salvation,
in quietness and trust is your strength."
ISAIAH 30:15

This verse sounds lovely. . .until you go on: "But you would have none of it."

These are the words Isaiah relayed to God's "obstinate children" (v. 1). They could just as easily be directed to any of us today. The words of the Lord speak of people who "carry out plans that are not [His]," and heap "sin upon sin" (v. 1). They are "children unwilling to listen to the LORD's instruction" (v. 9), who ask their prophets instead to "tell us pleasant things" (v. 10).

How easy it is to fall into the bad habit of relying on our own way! There are hundreds, maybe thousands, of books each year published with the sole purpose of helping us to help ourselves. They teach us to distract ourselves with compliments and inspirational fluff. God compares this kind of living to the creation of a wall that is cracked and bulging, not able to stand up under its own weight. So it collapses. Yet it doesn't just fall down. It crumbles into such a worthless heap that not even a bit of it is functional (vv. 12–14).

So, how do you fight this result? God gives us the answer. Through repentance and rest, quietness and trust. You won't find a better way to develop those qualities than through daily prayer.

Dear Lord, help me to trust You and to want
to see through Your eyes. Amen. —ML

GRACE

*When you have eaten and are
satisfied, praise the LORD your God for
the good land he has given you.*
DEUTERONOMY 8:10

Repetition can be a very good thing. For those of us who are grow-ing older, it can be the only way of hanging on to our memory of names, places, dates, our own birthday, and so on. Some people place a picture of a special person or event in a place where it can be seen regularly, and every day the picture serves as a reminder to be thankful for that person or opportunity.

How many times do you eat in a day? Three, maybe more? Do you pray each time before you eat? Maybe we should wait, as Deuteronomy 8 suggests, and pray afterward, thanking God for the blessings He has given to us.

Perhaps you aren't in the habit of praying at all with meals. However, there is definitely a reason for it. Moses points it out here in the following verses: "Be careful that you do not forget the LORD your God. . . . Otherwise, when you eat and are satisfied. . .then your heart will become proud and you will forget the LORD your God" (vv. 11–12, 14).

So use your mealtimes as reminders, as a picture of all the good opportunities God has given you. Eat, and remember. Drink, and remember. Be satisfied, and remember. Pray, and remember.

*Dear Lord, thank You for this food, and
for the people who made it, and for You,
who have made everything. —ML*

WORRIED SICK

*The mind governed by the flesh is death, but the
mind governed by the Spirit is life and peace.*
ROMANS 8:6

Do you worry? Ahem. Perhaps a new question is in order. What did you worry about today? This morning? In the last hour? Goodness knows there's enough in the news to drive people to bite every single nail off their poor hands, if they could only stop wringing them long enough to get a nibble.

Yet a life of worry is not the life our Father had in mind. It's not really a life at all. "The mind governed by the flesh is death." Here Paul is more likely speaking of a spiritual death, but a physical death is just as likely. A mind that is overcome by the body's physical desires and needs will not be a mind that can focus on the path to Christ. These desires and needs can produce mental distress (What will I eat?) or they can actually worry the mind to a frazzle, like a dog worrying a bone to a saliva-soaked, useless lump.

So what does this mean? Don't care about physical needs? Ignore our desires? Don't worry, be happy? No, just don't be ruled by these things. Don't let the striving for physical satisfaction or the emotional desire for calm cause you to neglect the daily maintenance of spiritual health.

The Spirit is life and peace. Pray daily for more of the Spirit and less of the flesh.

*Dear Lord, help me to trust in You and ask
You for all that I need. Amen.* —ML

THE
UNBELIEVER'S PRAYER

*The boy's father exclaimed, "I do believe;
help me overcome my unbelief!"*
MARK 9:24

This prayer could be called "The Parent's Prayer." Is this not the cry of every mother and father? Perhaps especially so for those who have children going through the suffering of chronic illness, mental illness, addiction, school struggles, and spiritual battles.

Let's be honest, none of us would want to deal with this father's struggle for more than an hour, let alone years. It's bad enough that his son has an unexplained condition that doesn't allow him to speak. Every parent knows the frustration of trying to figure out what a pre-speech toddler wants or doesn't want—generally while he's in the middle of a piercing scream that could wake the dead. Yet here is a child who periodically throws himself into harm's way—"into fire or water to kill him" (v. 22). We can guess who has been there every time to save his boy from being burned or drowned.

This father believes there is a cure, an answer. Why else would he come to see Jesus? At the same time, this man is tired. He has been disappointed so many times. It is not hard at all to understand his cry for help. Anne Brontë echoed this feeling in her poem "The Doubter's Prayer":

Without some glimmering in my heart,
I could not raise this fervent prayer;
But, oh! a stronger light impart,
And in Thy mercy fix it there.

Dear Lord, help me believe more. Amen. —ML

EXPOSED

He will bring to light what is hidden in
darkness and will expose the motives of the heart.
1 CORINTHIANS 4:5

Have you ever replaced lightbulbs in a room? Listen to the voice of experience: Don't do this while company is over. Suddenly every dust bunny, every finger smudge, every piece of lint, is exposed for all the world to see. No, it's better to do this well before your visitors arrive, so you have time to do something about it. Or just take the lightbulbs out again, light some candles, and call it mood lighting. Who cares if it's only four in the afternoon?

When would you like your secrets brought to light? In what setting would you like the motives of your heart laid bare? Why not ask God to reveal truth to you in the quiet and privacy of your own conversations with Him?

When you pray, ask God to bring to light the sins you have forgotten that day. Ask Him to point out things that you haven't even realized you are struggling with. Paul said, "My conscience is clear, but that does not make me innocent" (v. 4). Just because you think you are on the right path doesn't mean you've never taken a wrong step. Ask God to turn on the lights and reveal the weak points in your faith.

But then don't be surprised if what you see is a messy room!

Dear Lord, shine Your light on my heart so I
can be a better witness for You. Amen. —ML

LIKE A TREE

*Blessed is the one. . .whose delight is in the law of
the L*ORD*, and who meditates on his law day and night.*
PSALM 1:1–2

Sometimes the best thing you can do when you take time to be with
God is simply to meditate on His Word.

When you are tired, it is good to be reminded that His Word
endures. When you are weak, it is good to remember His Word is
strong. When you are confused, it is good to remember His Word
has answers. When you have been hurt, it is good to know His Word
can heal.

A tree has no choice about where it is rooted. Through a turn in
the wind or the whim of a bird or the thought of a gardener, a seed
is planted in the ground. Then, year after year, the tree grows there
(or doesn't). The tree cannot go for a walk or visit other grounds.
So a tree planted by streams of water is blessed indeed. That tree
gets the benefit of life-giving liquid along with the changing scenery
the stream brings under its boughs each day.

So a person who delights in God's Word is blessed by it. It gives
life, and it brings an unending array of characters and circumstances
to your mind, without you ever having to take a step. You can stand
strong in the knowledge of God's commands and still experience a
wealth of opportunities—and prosper!

Dear Lord, thank You for Your Word. Amen. —ML

NOT
YOUR BATTLE

"All those gathered here will know that it is not by sword or spear that the LORD saves; for the battle is the LORD's, and he will give all of you into our hands."
1 SAMUEL 17:47

Have you ever been involved in a really ugly fight? Harsh words are hurled on both sides, personal attacks are launched, people pick sides, and soon it seems your whole world is at war.

But that battle that you are fighting? It isn't yours. So lay down your weapons and squelch the fires of vengeance. Pack up your warhorses and get down on your knees instead.

David was in an ugly fight. Goliath was not exactly a humble opponent. He was big and loud and mean and scary. The Israelites were not showing themselves to be especially brave at the time. So David, the shepherd, stepped into the middle of this mess armed not with swords and catapults and spears, and not even with a sling and a stone. No, David was armed with the strength and power and might of the living God.

You are too. Perhaps you haven't seen God rescue you from the paw of a lion or bear, as David had. Yet you can be confident that God is more than able to get you through whatever challenge you are facing. Spend some time with Him. Ask Him to help you. Place your battle in His capable hands.

Dear Lord, please let me lean on You. Amen. —ML

PILLOW TALK

In peace I will lie down and sleep,
for you alone, LORD, make me dwell in safety.
PSALM 4:8

It's happened to the best of us. You wait until the house is all quiet to spend some time with the Lord. You grab your Bible; you get your notebook. Your pen is poised over the page as you wait on the Lord. You open your mouth a little as you begin your prayer. You breathe deeply and relax as you list the ways you are grateful that day for God's help and blessings.

Your Bible slips a little down your comforter. Your notebook pages crumple. Your pen rolls to the floor. Your mouth opens broadly as the snoring begins. You breathe deeply in heavenly sleep as you dream about God's blessings. . .or something like that.

A mind stilled in prayer can easily become a mind stilled by sleep. That's okay. At least, some of the time. You wouldn't want your prayer time to end up being nap time every day. Yet one of the benefits of a relationship with the Maker of heaven and earth is the peace that comes from nowhere else. It's better than any super-high-tech mattress or the latest ultra essential oil.

In the peace that comes with prayer, you can lie down and sleep, knowing God is watching over you.

You alone, Lord, make me dwell
in safety. Amen. —ML

ABBA

Because you are his sons, God sent the
Spirit of his Son into our hearts, the Spirit
who calls out, "Abba, Father."
GALATIANS 4:6

Did you have a special name for your father or grandfather when you were little? Perhaps it's a name you still use to this day. Saying that name can conjure up all kinds of memories—portraits of an intimate relationship with one you love, and who loves you.

God wants to have that same kind of close relationship with us. He loves us more tenderly and patiently than even the best of fathers here on earth. He has adopted us as His own, making us brothers and sisters of Jesus Christ. Jesus called out to His Father in the language of His childhood—Abba—so we can call on our Father God and expect the same intimacy.

Indeed, God has given us His Spirit to live within us. It's a mystery. Yet if you've ever been in a hard spot when you couldn't really think even how to pray, you have probably felt closer to understanding this mystery than at any other time. It's at those times you can almost hear the Spirit's voice whispering for you, calling on God on your behalf, asking for help when you can't even form the words.

How amazing that the Creator of the universe allows us to call Him "Daddy"!

Abba, Father, thank You for making
me Your child. Amen. —ML

THE ONE
WHO LIFTS

But you, LORD, are a shield around me,
my glory, the One who lifts my head high.
PSALM 3:3

Down. Depressed. Dejected. Droopy. In the dumps. Disappointed.
Some days there is no use trying to hide it. You are just sad. It may be something has happened recently to make you feel this way. It may be an old sorrow that has come to mind. For some, it may be no reason at all—just some concoction of chemicals in the brain is out of whack and your happy mood is the casualty.

Whatever it is, God is ready and willing to protect us from ourselves. Just read Psalms for a little while and you will see the psalmist was often not a happy camper. In fact, he could be a bit of a downer! At least he knew where to turn for help: "But you, LORD, are a shield around me, my glory, the One who lifts my head high."

God is able to lift up your spirit, your mood, your hopes, and even your chin. Remember to glory in Him, particularly when you are not feeling so glorious. He will answer. He will put a shield around you. He will absorb your sorrow and lift your head up out of the gloom.

Dear Lord, please help me to know
You are always with me, even on
my sad days. Amen. —ML

A PRAYER TO ARMS

*Finally, be strong in the
Lord and in his mighty power.*
EPHESIANS 6:10

Dear God, help me to know my real enemy—not my annoying neighbor, or my demanding boss, or my fickle friend. Help me to recognize the powers of this dark world when they come at me, and help me not to waste my time fretting over little offenses that mean nothing. Help me to think bigger, to see broader, to know more of Your wisdom.

Help me to stand my ground.

God, make my tongue speak Your truth. Wrap Your Word around me tight like a belt—help it to hold all things together. Please mold for me a guard around my heart, so that I can long to follow Your righteous path and not the desires of this world.

Make me ready, Lord, with answers to those who ask questions and wonder about You. Help me not be afraid to speak but to be confident in my replies because I know You are behind every word of the gospel of peace.

Make me strong so I can bear Your shield of faith, repelling insecurities and fears and doubts that are the weapons of my enemy. God, You know the words and thoughts and actions that sting me the most. Please help me let Your peace and the certainty of You be a salve on my soul.

*Fill my head and heart with Your Spirit so
I can go out and pierce others with the
security of salvation in You. Amen. —ML*

MORNING ROUTINE

*In the morning, LORD, you hear my voice; in the morning
I lay my requests before you and wait expectantly.*
PSALM 5:3

Dog owners are often greeted by their companions in the morning, with eyes full of expectation. The request of the dog is quite clear—take me on a walk, please! It is certain that dogs are the most energetic waiters in the animal kingdom. Even a well-trained dog, while seemingly sitting patiently, has every muscle fiber in its body just straining to be released. Why is this? Because they are certain, with not a shadow of a doubt, that very soon indeed they will be allowed out. They will be let go. They will be free to run.

Maybe you wait for the Lord's answers in the same way. But many of us do not. Do you ever lay requests before God morning after morning (or night after night), going through the routine, but not really believing God will come through?

Oh, to be like an expectant dog! Waiting for God's response to our prayers with eagerness and readiness to spring into whatever discipline or action God requires. Waiting with certainty, sure that our Father will answer soon. Waiting with utter trust in the Master, because we know He has our best interests always in mind. Waiting expectantly.

*Dear God, help me to have confidence
and faith to ask You anything, and to wait
eagerly for the reply. Amen. —ML*

WRONG NUMBER

*"Go and cry out to the gods you have chosen.
Let them save you when you are in trouble!"*
JUDGES 10:14

Reading the book of Judges is like watching some kind of soap opera for the nations. First the Israelites love God, and then they don't. Then they do. Then they don't. Then they do. . . . You get the picture.

Judges chapter 10 starts off calmly enough, but then we get to verse 6: "Again the Israelites did evil in the eyes of the LORD." Our writer then proceeds to list no less than seven different groups of gods that the Israelites decided to serve instead of the one and only Lord God. After the Israelites get crushed by the Ammonites (one of the people groups whose gods they were worshipping) and start feeling distressed, they suddenly remember to call on the only name that matters.

Does this sound familiar at all? Things are going pretty well. Your basic needs have been met and now you want more. So you start chasing after ways to get it: money, power, position, image, people, leisure, and insert-idol-name-here. Somewhere in the middle of that chasing you stop becoming a worshipper of God and start becoming a worshipper of other stuff. You forget who you are. You forget who to call on.

Thanks be to our merciful Savior, who is always there for us. Even when we call the wrong number.

*Dear God, thank You for loving me even when
I'm unfaithful to You. I'm so sorry. Amen. —ML*

SUCCESS

*Then he prayed, "LORD, God of my master
Abraham, make me successful today, and
show kindness to my master Abraham."*
GENESIS 24:12

How often do you pray for job success? Perhaps a promotion or a raise or some sort of recognition?

How often do you pray for God to show kindness to your boss?

Imagine if the CEO of a corporation sent his top executive out on a matchmaking mission for his own son! That would seem like a fairly trivial matter in today's business terms. Back in the age of Abraham, the family *was* the business. So Abraham sent his most important servant—the one in charge of everything he owned (which was a lot, in those days)—on this very important mission. This servant is the only one he could trust to do the significant and delicate negotiation required to obtain a good wife for his son, who would carry on the family business.

The servant knew the weight of his responsibility. He wanted to do well, not just for himself, but for his master and his master's family. So he prayed. He asked God to help select the right woman for Isaac. God did not let him down.

Next time you are handed an important mission, remember to ask the ultimate CEO for help. Ask to do well, not just for yourself, but for your boss and for the whole company. God will not let you down.

*Dear God, thank You for good work
and the will to do it. Amen. —ML*

FLOOD

The Lord has heard my weeping.
PSALM 6:8

Flash flood alert. Psalm 6 has a rather high humidity level. The psalmist is in anguish, down to the bone. He has flooded his bed with tears and drenched his couch. Next thing you know, his friends will be filling up sandbags around him.

We've all been there. Something happens that just breaks your world apart, and the tears start coming. Then they won't stop. You think they will never stop. You think you will just go on weeping until you haven't a drop of water left in you, at which point you will be so overcome with dehydration, you will just die. Then what?

Isn't it somehow comforting to see the psalmist throwing himself on his couch in utter misery? To know that thousands of years ago, bad days—really horrible ones—happened? To know that in the end, the same Lord and God who soothed and saved that poor, miserable, soaking wet psalmist lying on his couch is the same Lord and God who soothes you today?

Our God is an expert on human suffering. He's had centuries of experience in counseling people through grief of all kinds. So next time you feel like the tears just won't ever stop, come immediately to the door of the best counselor you could ever find. Come in prayer. Come with a box of tissues. Just come.

Dear God, thank You for hearing my sobs
and not turning away. Amen. —ML

WATCHING FROM THE REEDS

*Then she placed the child in it and put it
among the reeds along the bank of the Nile.*

Exodus 2:3

There is very little emotion captured in the story of baby Moses. A woman has a baby. She can't hide him from the cruel government, which legislated his death, so she puts him in a basket in the river. No tears. No sound. The end.

It wasn't the end, thankfully, for baby Moses. It's hard to imagine that was the end for his mother either. Even after her daughter followed the baby boy, watching him be rescued by royalty; even after she finished nursing her son and gave him back to be raised by his adoptive family; even after the boy had grown up and fled the land—it seems likely that it wasn't the end of the story for Moses' mother.

How many mothers are there out there who have watched from the reeds and prayed? First, that their babies might be rescued, might be saved from whatever terrible set of circumstances they were born into, and might be given a chance to grow and live. Then, that their babies might continue to thrive, to become healthy adults. Maybe one day, to know that their mothers loved them.

Say a prayer today for those mothers watching from the reeds.

*Dear Lord, thank You for the gift of life. Please
bless all those mothers who have made sacrifices
so their babies could survive. Amen.* —ML

THE PIT OF NEGATIVITY

*Whoever digs a hole and scoops
it out falls into the pit they have made.*
PSALM 7:15

Sometimes those hoarder shows on television are fascinating, though disturbing, to watch. It's amazing to listen to and observe people who have almost dug their own graves. The walls made of stuff are literally falling in on them. Their lives are held together by piles of old memories, regrets, longings, and disappointments. The need to be filled by something they cannot find has left them empty, while their houses are stuffed to the rafters.

Any one of us can get stuck in the pit of negativity. It's so easy to do. One self-pitying thought leads to another, which then leads to an irritation with others, which leads to more exclusion, which leads to more jealousy, which leads to more irritation and isolation, and the cycle continues.

Instead of digging holes, let us work to help each other out of them. Let's give thanks for what we have, instead of counting what we don't. Through our prayers and worship, "sing the praises of the name of the LORD Most High" (v. 17). It's very hard to dig a hole if you keep looking up.

*Dear Lord, help me to not get trapped
by negative thoughts. Fill me with
Your Spirit. Amen.* —ML

WANT. ASK. GET.

You do not have because you do not ask God.
JAMES 4:2

It seems so simple. Want. Ask. Get. James breaks it down for us. He says, "You want something but don't get it. You kill and covet, but you cannot have what you want. You quarrel and fight. You do not have, because you do not ask God" (v. 2).

What is it you are afraid to ask for? What is it you are afraid to admit you need? Maybe you just need help. Maybe you need the truth. Maybe you need a loan. Maybe you need to be saved. Maybe you need to let go.

Want. Ask. Get.

What is it you really want? Not just a new car or more money or a nice outfit. What is it you're lacking that makes you want what others have? Do you want what God wants for you? Do you even know?

Once you know what you want, how do you ask? Do you look everywhere else first before coming to God? Do you go to Him right away? Do you come to Him humbly or as someone entitled?

You want, you ask—did you get it? If your answer's no, have you thought about why? What were your motivations? What's your reaction to not getting what you want?

If your answer is yes, have you thanked God? Have you shared what you have? Want. Ask. Get. Then give.

*Dear God, help me to make Your desires
for my life my own. Amen. —ML*

BARGAIN

*It is better not to make a vow than
to make one and not fulfill it.*

ECCLESIASTES 5:5

"God, if You just give me a puppy, I'll be good my whole life." How many children must have prayed a prayer like this one? How many of us are still praying this kind of prayer?

People make promises to God for all kinds of reasons, but most likely the biggest one of those reasons has to be to strike a deal. "God, if You'll _____, I will _____."

It is good to think of God as your friend. It is dangerous to think of God as your haggling partner.

Besides, He would be the worst person ever to bargain with. Why? He doesn't need anything. When you are trying to strike a deal, it's best to know what your counterpart needs—what they lack that you can offer.

The God who made time, who spun the earth into motion and placed the stars in the sky, does not need you. He does not need anything you have to offer. He does not need your promises. Especially the empty ones.

He does want you to come to Him. He does want to be near you. He does want to love you. He will give you everything you could ever need. Come near to God and He will come near to you. Not to negotiate a deal, but just to know Him more.

*Dear Father, if You'll love me, I will have
everything I need. Amen. —ML*

HELPER OF THE FATHERLESS

But you, God, see the trouble of the afflicted; you consider their grief and take it in hand. The victims commit themselves to you; you are the helper of the fatherless.

PSALM 10:14

Too many children know this grief—the gut-wrenching sorrow of losing a dad. Some have watched their fathers suffer and die. Some have watched their fathers walk away. In either case, the hole that is left behind is gaping.

Losing a parent shakes a person's foundations. Both sons and daughters feel this loss keenly, though perhaps somewhat differently. For sons, it is the loss of a role model, a strength giver, a provider, a teacher. For many daughters, losing a father means all of that, but also losing the first and perhaps the only man in the world who would truly love them no matter what. The one man who would always look at them—no matter how many pounds were on or off, or if it was a bad hair day, or if a pimple had erupted—and say with absolute honesty, "You are beautiful."

God sees your troubles, and He knows your pain. When you come to Him in prayer, He cradles you in the palm of His hand because He is that big. Big enough to take on your sorrow. Big enough to lift us all. Yet close enough and gentle enough to wipe your tears and whisper, "You are beautiful."

Father God, thank You for never leaving me. Please hold on tight. Amen. —ML

HUMBLED

*We all, like sheep, have gone astray, each
of us has turned to our own way; and the
Lord has laid on him the iniquity of us all.*
ISAIAH 53:6

When you come to God in prayer, do you ever feel the complete humbleness of your situation? It is a truly humiliating experience—not that God makes us feel how little we are, but that being near God makes us see how little we are.

Perhaps that's why we don't do it as often as we should. It's not comfortable to feel shame.

We are sheep. We run away. We ramble. We get off track. We lose our way. We chase after the wrong things. We fear everything. We cry out and complain. We can't find our way home. We are stubborn. We don't see well. We don't ask for help. We stumble.

Our Lord and Shepherd knows all of this and loves us still. He knows all of our wrongs, and He doesn't just forget them or wipe them away. He pays for them. In blood.

That is the God to whom you say your bedtime prayers.

*Dear God, I am humbled in Your presence. Help me
to live a life that is worthy of Your love. Amen. —ML*

WHAT TO DO?

*"When the foundations are being
destroyed, what can the righteous do?"*
PSALM 11:3

Anyone who has ever owned an old house knows what a worry a cracked foundation can be. Sometimes it can be repaired. But a foundation that is weak means the whole house will likely have to come down, or else it will eventually fall down.

The psalmist in Psalm 11 asks a good question. What can the righteous do? When the whole stability of a world is crumbling, when the people who are supposed to be upright are being corrupted, when everything that is supposed to be true turns out to be false—what can the righteous do? What should they do?

We might come up with many answers. Worry. Shout. Look for someone to blame. Use the trouble as an excuse to give up. Hurry up and build a new house.

But the psalmist doesn't tell the righteous what to do. He tells them where to look. "The LORD is in his holy temple; the LORD is on his heavenly throne" (v. 4).

When the foundations are shaken, look to the one who cannot be shaken. Look to the Lord, who is "righteous, he loves justice; the upright will see his face" (v. 7). Turn your face to God and ask for His help. Turn your eyes toward Him, and remember who is in control.

*Dear Lord, help me in times of trouble to
remember to turn to You in prayer. Amen. —ML*

FORMING

We are the clay, you are the potter;
we are all the work of your hand.
ISAIAH 64:8

People have a romantic vision of the potter: The potter spins the clay on the wheel, and a few moments later, a beautiful pot is formed. Voila!

But anyone who has worked with clay or watched a potter knows it's not that easy. Here's how it might go: The potter puts a slimy lump of clay on the wheel. The potter spins the wheel. The potter uses fingers and hands to start forming the lump. A beautiful shape begins to appear. The vase starts stretching up, up, and then—oh no! It folds over in a sad, twisted bow.

The potter begins again. The vase stretches up, and then, well, a little over. A little up. A little more over. The potter sighs in frustration, squashes the crooked vase, and starts again.

The ball forms into a bowl. The potter's hands smooth the rim of the bowl. The potter sneezes. A large dent appears in the rim of the bowl. The potter stops the wheel and goes to get a cup of coffee.

We are the clay. Thankfully, we are in the hands of a perfect potter. Yet the process of our spiritual formation can still be frustrating and longer than we wish. It will take daily prayer and lots of patience for us to wait and stretch up and up and up—into a functional vessel.

Dear Lord, may my prayers help me to
be formed by You. Amen. —ML

TRANSFORMING

And we all, who with unveiled faces contemplate the Lord's glory, are being transformed into his image with ever-increasing glory, which comes from the Lord, who is the Spirit.

2 CORINTHIANS 3:18

If you are like most people, you will find fault with at least one aspect of your image. It's hard to find anyone who is completely happy with the person she sees in the mirror.

It would be harder still to find anyone who is completely happy with the person she is—with all the decisions and thoughts and actions she has made in her life. Or even just today.

Thanks be to God, "where the Spirit of the Lord is, there is freedom" (v. 17). No one has to hide from the Lord. No one has to worry about the exterior image. No one has to feel alone.

If you have been running away from God for a while, or just neglecting your prayer life, it's time to turn and face Him. He does not expect you to be perfect. He expects that you will need transforming. He is happy to perform that work. He wants to shape you into the best human being you can be. Come and kneel before Him; don't hide your face. He can see through any veil you might try to wear anyway. Come and stand before His image and ask Him to transform you.

Dear God, I'm not happy with who I am. Please mold me into the person You want me to be. Amen. —ML

HOW YOU
SHOULD PRAY

"When you pray, do not be like the hypocrites."
MATTHEW 6:5

There are not that many places in the Bible that spell out exactly how people should perform the Christian disciplines of faith. Jesus' words in Matthew's Gospel come as a welcome relief to those who are seeking to know exactly how to behave as a follower of Christ.

First, He paints a picture of what not to do. Don't pray to be seen. Don't use prayer as a step on the faith success ladder. Don't think you have to be seen for the Father to hear your words. Don't look for any reward or praise outside of the glory that comes from God Himself.

Do not babble on, using words as a weapon of power or as a show of strength. Don't think that God desires quantity over quality. Don't make the mistake of thinking God needs to hear you speak at all.

Instead, pray quietly. Pray on your own. Pray in private. Pray with words that show God respect, that show you know His power. Thank God for His provision. Ask Him to forgive what you lack. Request His guidance and His salvation. Ask Him for His will to be done, even if you have no idea what that is just yet.

Then go out and live as you pray. Be forgiving, knowing your Father has forgiven you, time and time again, for all the small and big ways you have stumbled.

Our Father in heaven, let Your will
be done. Amen. —ML

FAST

"When you fast, do not look somber."
MATTHEW 6:16

People engage in all kinds of fasting fads these days. Juice fasts. Cleansing fasts. TV fasts. Fasting has become a status symbol of sorts. It's a true sign of a society that has plenty that people have the option to choose what they will declare as a fast.

For other people in the world, fasting is sadly just a way of life.

Yet fasting was meant to be a kind of prayer. The idea is to deliberately go without something (usually food) in order to focus on God and on His will for your life. It's a time to be reminded of who provides everything we eat and drink. It's a time to be reminded who we depend on and who we can trust with all of our needs and desires. Often it is meant to be a time to bring a particular desire or concern before God.

The fasting is not for God. It is not a show for others. The fasting is a very personal decision to engage in a small act of sacrifice and, in so doing, remind yourself of the much greater sacrifice God has made for you.

So if you do fast, don't make a show of it. Don't advertise it. Do it with a right heart and mind, and God will certainly honor your efforts.

Dear God, help me to focus on You more, no matter what else is going on in my life. Amen. —ML

FAITHFUL

If we are faithless, he remains faithful,
for he cannot disown himself.
2 TIMOTHY 2:13

Is there anyone who has not been unfaithful at one time or another? Not to a spouse or dating partner, or even a friend—not that kind of unfaithful. Perhaps there are people who have remained true in all of those situations.

But unfaithful to God—has anyone managed to escape that label? It seems unlikely. For many of us, the challenge would be to find a time when we *aren't* unfaithful. Even one whole day when we remain focused on His will—when we take charge of our thought life and of all our actions and remain obedient to Him every hour. When we remember to praise Him and thank Him for what He has given. When we don't get distracted by other objects of our desire—idols we have worshipped before.

God is gracious. He is faithful—forever faithful. He cannot deny Himself, and thus, He cannot deny His love for us. He will always be there for us, even when we stray far, far away. If we come to Him in prayer, He will always respond. For that, we can be thankful. For that, we should be faithful.

Gracious God, thank You for always
being true to us, even though we
are not worthy. Amen. —ML

MARY'S GLORY

*"He has been mindful of
the humble state of his servant."*
LUKE 1:48

What is striking about Mary's prayer in Luke 1 is the confidence.
Here is Mary, a young girl in a completely unheard-of situation. She
is carrying the child of God in her womb. Strange and wonderful
things are happening around her. People are having experiences
and dreams and hearing from God in ways they never have. Mary
receives Elizabeth's blessing with all the composure of a woman
five times her age.

It is clear to see this confidence does not come through the mind
of a teenager, ruled by emotions and hormones. It comes from a
deeper place. "My soul glorifies the Lord and my spirit rejoices in
God my Savior" (vv. 46–47). Mary knew she was not anything special
on her own. She knew also, from deep within, that God was doing
something great, not just for her, but for generations. In the same
way she had heard as a child the stories of the amazing things He
had done for her ancestors, she could see with certainty the Lord's
hand at work now in her own time, her own village, her own body.

Let us come to God and praise Him with the same certainty
Mary had. Let us read His Word and remember His marvelous
works. Then let us pray with a humble heart and ask Him to open
our eyes to the work He is doing today, in our world, in ourselves.

My soul glorifies You, my Lord. Amen. —ML

WHAT ARE
YOUR GIFTS?

*Each of you should use whatever gift you
have received to serve others, as faithful
stewards of God's grace in its various forms.*
1 PETER 4:10

Were you born an artist? A painter, writer, or sculptor? Do you gravitate toward the sciences? Are you gifted in sports? Floral arranging? Speaking? Computers? Sales? Building? Organizing? There are so many talents.

What about your spiritual gifts—such as teaching, prophesying, showing mercy, serving others, encouragement, and leadership?

Some people are confused about their abilities, and they might even think they have been passed over when the Almighty was giving out gifts. Yet, we can be assured that everyone has been given talents, and everyone is expected to use them.

If you are questioning what yours are—ask God. The Lord will be more than pleased to tell you. Asking for His guidance concerning our talents and spiritual gifts is also wisdom, since God wants us to use them with a servant's heart. Even though that notion might seem old-fashioned within our modern mindset, it is how Jesus conducted Himself—with the heart of a servant—when He walked among us.

*God, thank You for the gifts and abilities You have
blessed me with. Help me not to waste them or use
them for my own gain but to serve others with my
talents in order to glorify Your name. Amen. —AH*

WHEN PRAYER
SEEMS IMPOSSIBLE

LORD, save us! LORD, grant us success!
Blessed is he who comes in the name of the LORD.
From the house of the LORD we bless you.
PSALM 118:25–26

Sometimes the last thing on earth we feel like doing is praying.

We're angry. We're scared. We're exhausted. We're world weary.

Maybe we've just had an argument with a close friend. Maybe we've just been admitted to the hospital with yet another debilitating illness. Maybe we are bone tired from working two jobs and still not making the rent. Maybe we feel as though our prayers are never heard. That we are truly alone. That life seems hopeless.

What in the world do we do?

Pray.

Yes, even then. The book of Psalms is full of every manner of heart-cry to the Almighty. Nothing is held back. Every tear is shed in those passages. Every weary thought is revealed. Every doubt and misery expressed. And what happened? God listened. He came near. He became the people's rescuer and redeemer. As in Bible times, God may not choose to lift us out of every storm; but when we cry out, He will be there with us, whether it's in a howling gale or still, blue sea.

Prayer is mighty because the one to whom we pray is mighty. Let us never forget.

Savior, please be with me in my hour of
need and bring me hope. Amen. —AH

I WILL
GIVE YOU REST

The LORD replied, "My Presence will go
with you, and I will give you rest."
EXODUS 33:14

The world is full of clamor and shouts and unsavory whispers. Our attention is stolen at every turn. Even Christians can absorb and reflect the noise if they're not careful. They can take in that frenzy, that panic. That soul-wrenching fright.

Christ did not come to give us a spirit of fear. He came not to condemn but to save. He came to give us a rich life in spirit and truth. He came with healing in His hands. He came with redemption and mercy, love most abundant.

Let us rest in these truths—rest in Him.

The Lord reaches out to you. He will take you by your outstretched hand and lead you to a restful place. By still waters that lap gently to the shore. A place that is far from the roaring crowds. Far from the clamor of fear. From the whispers of temptation. From the accusing cries of the enemy.

Yes, the Lord says, "My Presence will go with you, and I will give you rest."

Can you hear His gentle voice? He's calling us to sit awhile. To visit. To rest.

Father, amid my trials and frustrations today,
give me rest and peace in You. No matter
how difficult my circumstances may be, help
me to remember that You are more than
capable and sufficient for me. Amen. —AH

CHAPEL BELLS, TOLLING FOR THEE

*"They sing to the music of timbrel and lyre;
they make merry to the sound of the pipe."*
JOB 21:12

Stained-glass, arched windows and a steeple adorn a pure white chapel on a distant hill. How beautiful. How peaceful. How heartening. And the bells, oh how pretty are those chapel bells that ring out through the vales and through the villages to gladden every heart who hears their music.

It is a reminder to see beyond the mundane. Downturned faces will once again rise from the daily tedium and toil and witness the firmament—the swirling clouds, azure sky, and stars of night that shout His glory!

The tolling bells call to me and to you—as a reminder to gather together in worship, to seek, to fellowship, to share communion, to praise, to pray. To return to all the things—and the one—that are too easily forgotten, too easily set aside.

The bells ring of hope. Those in Christ have great reason to make merry, to shout in joy, to sing to the music of all kinds of instruments.

When we hear the chapel bells, let us remember to look up. To gather in worship. To raise our voices in song. To embrace the hope. And to prayerfully and excitedly share that hope with all who will listen.

*Lord, You are worthy of all praise. I want
to worship You every day, every hour,
and every moment. Amen.* —AH

SWEET TO
THE SOUL

If we confess our sins, he is faithful
and just and will forgive us our sins and
purify us from all unrighteousness.
1 John 1:9

A boy sneaks a big sugar cookie from Mom's cookie jar just before suppertime.

Does the boy sit at the table, calmly looking around, innocently munching on the sweet treat?

Probably not.

Most likely—since he knows his mother asked him not to eat a cookie before dinner because she loves him and wants him to eat a healthy dinner first—the boy will do what many boys do and hide in his room with his guilty pleasure.

The boy's mother—since she already knows about the incident, because she really does have eyes in the back of her head—hopes that he will confess his folly. Would it really be that hard to come to her and say, "I'm sorry, Mom. I shouldn't have eaten the cookie. Will you forgive me?"

Repentance may feel uncomfortable, but only for a short time. Usually Mom will forgive with a gentle warning and a hug.

God's love is far beyond our own, so we are safe in His perfect justice and mercy. We need not run and hide in our folly but go to Him instead. He is faithful and just and will forgive us our sins. Yes, repentance is such sweetness to the soul.

Father God, I come to You now with all my sins,
both intentional and unintentional. Thank You
for Your unlimited grace. Amen. —AH

PRIDE IS A WILY BEAST

Better to be lowly in spirit along with the oppressed than to share plunder with the proud.
PROVERBS 16:19

We've seen it. We've experienced it. It makes our hearts shudder. *Pride.*

Pride doesn't sweep in on a cloud of French perfume. Pride slithers in brazenly, yet craftily, and is as pleasant to endure as breathing deeply from the mouth of an open grave. Oh my! That image offends our more delicate sensibilities. But so does pride, which can settle itself into our spirits—if we allow it to—as we relish good fortune such as money, accolades, physical beauty, knowledge, fame, etc.

These potential conduits of arrogance seem obvious, but pride is a wily beast, since the opposite of good fortune can conjure it up just as easily. We can choose haughtiness when we know we've risen victorious in our suffering. When we know we are able to endure—even invite—great hardship and lack. You mean we can choose to feel prideful in poverty? Yes, it can come when we least expect it and for any reason. That's why pride is so sly as well as insidious. In the book of Proverbs, God says that He detests the proud of heart.

Uh-oh. Not good. Then how can anyone cleanse oneself from this putrid pride?

With the power of God through prayer. He will cleanse us from all unrighteousness, including pride, and the results will smell sweeter than the finest French perfume.

God, take me down from my pedestal and teach me the meaning of true humility. Amen. —AH

LOOKING
FOR TROUBLE

Finally, brothers and sisters, whatever is true,
whatever is noble, whatever is right, whatever is pure,
whatever is lovely, whatever is admirable—if anything
is excellent or praiseworthy—think about such things.
PHILIPPIANS 4:8

Here's the scene. . . .

You have lunch with your dear friend, Tallulah, and you both are having a nice time together, chatting about all the latest news in each other's lives. The usual catching-up stuff. Then you hug and say goodbye. Yet on your way home, your mind begins to pick apart—every—single—word—that was said during your lunch. You pick and pick like a vulture—until you rise up from the now-dead carcass of a luncheon—with a morsel of questionable meat. Ah-ha! Yes, you now know positively that Tallulah has slighted you in some way with something she said at lunch. Or might have said. Or might have meant. Maybe.

We women are notorious with this pick-pick thing. Are we not? The bottom line is, if we're looking for trouble, we will find it. Guaranteed. That's life. So, instead of picking, let us give each other one of the best friendship gifts—the benefit of the doubt. Let us pray this beautiful Philippians scripture aloud.

Whatever is true, whatever is noble, whatever
is right, whatever is pure, whatever is lovely,
whatever is admirable—if anything is excellent
or praiseworthy—Lord, please allow me to
think about such things. Amen. —AH

HOW BEAUTIFUL
IS THY NAME!

All flocks and herds, and the animals of the
wild, the birds in the sky, and the fish in the sea,
all that swim the paths of the seas. LORD, our Lord,
how majestic is your name in all the earth!
PSALM 8:7–9

When we experience an alpine walk along a misty trail. Or take in the moon's reflection on a still, blue sea. When we hear the thunderous roar of a lion or the voice of the wind through swaying palms. Or when we see the ballet of the dolphins or the glistening fire of a rare gem or the artwork in the plumage of a peacock, don't we feel a rush of awe? Don't we feel a sweet ache in our hearts to be thankful—to someone?

God's creation is indeed full of beauty and wonder, and we should take great pleasure in His handiwork. We should explore His world. We should see with new eyes each morning. To delight in everything, from the smallest of snowflake designs to the vaulting cliffs on the grandest mountains.

As Christians we do not worship creation but instead worship the one who is the Creator of such magnificence. A thankful heart full of praise is a form of prayer. Shall we thank Him and praise Him today?

Lord, our Lord, how majestic is Your name in all the earth!

Creator God, thank You for the beauty and
wonder of Your handiwork. Give me grateful
eyes to see it every day. Amen. —AH

DON'T
FORGET TO SMILE

*"By this everyone will know that you
are my disciples, if you love one another."*
JOHN 13:35

Religious bondage. Maybe you know some folks who are suffering with this spiritual ailment. They're the ones who are so busy wringing their hands that they forgot to raise them in praise. If someone is hungry and asks for bread, they're the ones who divvy out a stone, because the stone will help the needy learn endurance. They're also the ones who forgot how to laugh or smile or encourage, because they're obsessed with trying to make certain that no one breaks a rule. Ever.

Yes, you guessed it—they're the prune gang.

Oh dear. Sounds like the same pharisaical struggles in Bible times. What about the unbelievers in our midst? What will they think? Who wants a faith that looks oppressive? They'll be lacing up their running shoes to get away from us as fast as possible! As Christians we should indeed follow Christ in all things; but that prayerful following should cause us to want to reflect His joy, peace, and love, which He gives freely to us.

If the joy in our hearts is so uncontainable that it's busy spreading itself all over our faces, people will take off their running shoes and stay to chat with us. They'll ask, "What is it that makes you smile?"

*Jesus, just as You love me, help me to love
everyone around me—family, friends, and
foes. I want to be a perfect reflection of
You to a hurting world. Amen. —AH*

WE'RE
MEANT TO FLY

"Come now, let us settle the matter," says the
LORD. "Though your sins are like scarlet, they
shall be as white as snow; though they are
red as crimson, they shall be like wool."
ISAIAH 1:18

Suppose there was a beautiful white seagull that suddenly got caught in a patch of sticky mud, but the more the poor thing struggled to fly, the more the mire coated its wings and held it down. Got that image in your imagination?

How is that different from our daily walk on this earth? We as humans were meant to fly free of worry and disease and suffering and death. This fallen journey is not what God had planned for us, but it was instigated by humanity through the choice that God gave us—which is free will. Our spirits weren't meant for these immense burdens. They are almost unbearable at times.

Wow. Sounds pretty hopeless. It is completely hopeless without the love and sacrifice of Jesus. Only He can fulfill the promise in scripture that says He will make our sins, which are scarlet, as white as snow. No one else can do it. No other gods. Not our own desperate efforts at redemption. Nothing.

His promise is real, and with His redemption comes freedom. It's like being released from the mire—yes, clean and white, wings outstretched, and soaring!

What will your prayerful reply be to His promise? His redemption?

Jesus, thank You for Your priceless sacrifice
on the cross for my sins. Help me to soar
free from the taint of sin. Amen. —AH

WORDS GONE BAD

*May these words of my mouth and this
meditation of my heart be pleasing in your
sight, LORD, my Rock and my Redeemer.*

PSALM 19:14

There's a fuzzy, ripe peach in the grocery store, and it has your name on it. It's juicy, fragrant, and sweet as candy. You tenderly bring it home and set it in the bottom of your crisper in the fridge. And then you promptly forget about it.

That same luscious fuzzy peach will soon be covered over with the ugliest and fuzziest green monster-mold you have ever seen, making it impossible to eat. Impossible for anything of good use. That is the way of words gone bad.

Once our words are spoken, once they have tumbled out of our mouths, we can never get them back. They are like the water that plunges from a cliff into the sea. It just keeps on going, flowing and changing everything it touches. That water cannot come back. Our words cannot come back into our mouths. Yes, we can apologize and make amends. We can ask the Lord to forgive us, and He will keep His promise. Yet the sting of those thoughtless remarks can sometimes last a lifetime—in the recipient's heart as well as in our own spirits.

A helpful daily prayer would be to ask the Lord to temper our words with wisdom and love. That what we say will not go bad like a rotten piece of fruit. But that our words will be pleasing and good and usable in His sight!

*God, help my words to always be kind,
compassionate, and uplifting. Amen.* —AH

NO SHRINKING VIOLETS HERE

"Have I not commanded you? Be strong and courageous. Do not be afraid; do not be discouraged, for the LORD your God will be with you wherever you go."
JOSHUA 1:9

When the world says, "Boo," do you jump? It's very hard not to. Right? Our days can be arduous, and our nights riddled with terrors. Our spirits grow bone weary and our hearts skittish and faint. So, when people mean to harm us or Satan comes to attack us, we feel like running to hide in a safe little closet or crawling in bed and pulling the covers over our heads for a day.

Or a month.

Until we sense that life has decided to settle down. But the problem is, just as soon as the wave of suffering is over, we see another storm brewing on the horizon. How can we ride these relentless storms for a lifetime and make it safely to the shores of heaven?

Reading God's Word, staying connected to a Bible-believing church, and praying are the only answers in these perilous times. If we remain faithful to following Christ, we will be able to rise up and say to the world with confidence, "Lord, I will be courageous. I will not fear what the world can do to me. I will not become discouraged, since I know You will be with me wherever I go."

Father, I have complete victory through You.
With You on my side, I have nothing to fear.
Help me to fully trust in You. Amen. —AH

DO YOU EVER FEEL LIKE A MISFIT?

For here we do not have an enduring city,
but we are looking for the city that is to come.
HEBREWS 13:14

Do you ever feel as though you don't fit in anywhere? That you're not in sync with the rest of the world? That somehow the earth and its inhabitants are singing a tune you've never even heard of?

Well, that can be a good thing. We are not intended for this world. Our home is meant to be in heaven with God. Reunited with the one who made us, who loves us best.

Yet we certainly try to fit in down here, don't we? We don the finest costumes, whatever is in style. We engage in the most practiced and acceptable-sounding banter—the popular vernacular of the day. Yes, sometimes we find ourselves dancing to the tune of a fallen earth, which might even include the transgressions we witness all around us.

This city or town or country village of ours is not a forever place for us. As Christians, we are not of this world. We are only passing through. So, the next time you feel as though you don't belong here, know that in a way, it couldn't be truer.

We are longing for home, the home where we will fit perfectly, and the home that will never pass away. Shall we pray for others— that they too will find their true home?

God, comfort me when I feel alone and lost in this
forsaken world. You are my true home. Amen. —AH

HE HOLDS
THE BLUEPRINT

*"And even the very hairs of
your head are all numbered."*
MATTHEW 10:30

We spend our lives searching for someone to understand us, to "get" us. Don't we? When we find it, what a blessing! Yet the understanding we long for comes freely from the Almighty. Even though there are billions of humans on our planet, no two people are just alike. Not even identical twins. We each are uniquely and wonderfully made. It is our loving Creator who holds that blueprint—which He considers precious—that has your name on it.

Imagine God so loving the world—loving *us*—that His "knowing" extends to the number of hairs on our heads? He knows every single thing about us. The kind of friends we enjoy. Our favorite ice cream, favorite pets, and favorite hobbies. The things that tickle our funny bones. The things that make us cry at the movies. Every secret we've hidden. Our deepest longings. Our worst nightmares. Yes, the Lord knows every nuance and detail about us. He loves us dearly.

Knowing these truths will help us to pray, since being loved and understood by the one to whom we are praying makes all the difference in the way we begin, "Dear Lord. . ."

*Thank You for knowing and loving every single
part of me. Help me to run to You when I feel
misunderstood or forgotten. Amen. —AH*

THE WAY WE
WERE CREATED TO BE

*And do not grieve the Holy Spirit of God, with
whom you were sealed for the day of redemption.
Get rid of all bitterness, rage and anger, brawling
and slander, along with every form of malice.
Be kind and compassionate to one another, forgiving
each other, just as in Christ God forgave you.*
EPHESIANS 4:30–32

As Christians, we have been given a promise of eternal life; but
even as Christians, we can still grieve the Holy Spirit who lives
within us. When we explode at our husband and then let the sun
go down on that anger. When we say slanderous things about our
neighbor. When we make plans that have malicious intent. When
we hold bitterness in our heart toward our best friend. All of these
transgressions—and, well, any kind of sin—grieve the Holy Spirit.
Why? He is perfect love. He loves us enough to help us out of our
wayward thoughts and our errant ways. To be perfected in our faith.
To be made whole and beautiful.

What a wonderful prayer today, and every day, that the Holy Spirit
will make us more like Him. Ah, yes, the way we were created to be!

*Holy Spirit, please don't allow my sinful nature to get
in the way of Your transforming, sanctifying power.
Embolden me to spread the gospel and love the
unlovable. Align me with Your will. Amen. —AH*

WHERE
SHALL I PRAY?

*But Jesus often withdrew
to lonely places and prayed.*
LUKE 5:16

Are you searching for the best place to talk to God? One might think of a great cathedral or perhaps a hometown chapel. Or maybe you'd like to be near a quiet stream or sitting under a favorite willow tree with the breeze giving sway to the leaves. What about one's front porch early in the morning before everyone rises or the solitary space of a prayer closet? Fortunately, all of these places work, because God is omnipresent. Since the Lord is all around us, He can hear our pleas and our praises wherever we happen to be. In a crowded bus or a stadium full of people or even an airport terminal bustling with noisy travelers.

We know from God's Word that Jesus often withdrew to quiet places to pray. The culture during Jesus' time—even without anything fast-paced or high-tech—could still have created enough "busy" to make seeking out a solitary place important. Vital, really.

So, even though we can pray anywhere and everywhere, let us also seek out solitary places to talk to God. We can regain our sense of peace—His peace. To hear His words of guidance. To remember that His power is sufficient for every day, every task.

Where is your favorite quiet place to talk to God?

*Lord, help me to carve out pockets of time to seek
You in quiet, solitary prayer. You deserve my
complete, undivided attention. Amen.* —AH

A FACE
LIT WITH JOY

*Do not be anxious about anything, but in every
situation, by prayer and petition, with thanksgiving,
present your requests to God. And the peace of
God, which transcends all understanding, will
guard your hearts and your minds in Christ Jesus.*
PHILIPPIANS 4:6–7

Sometimes when we bow our heads, we feel a little hesitant in addressing God, knowing He is the Creator of all things. It's certainly not the same as approaching our earthly father, or our boss, or our teacher or pastor. So, we sometimes approach God with trepidation.

Fortunately, God's Word gives us direction, even in prayer. First, we are not to spend our lives wringing our hands in worry. If we have concerns and requests, we should present them to God and trust Him with the answer. His response might not be what we asked for or on our timetable, but He will be faithful, because He loves us.

We are also to make our appeals with a thankful heart, rather than with a muttering and grumbling spirit, since the Lord is good and He knows how to give good gifts to His children. When we follow these divine instructions, the Lord will give us peace, a peace that is beyond human understanding. It is the kind of calm and sweet serenity that will make all those who meet us ask, "What gives your heart courage, and what is it that makes your face light up with joy?"

*Lord, I surrender to You every worry,
fear, and burden. You are more than
sufficient for me. Amen. —AH*

HIS WAYS

*Therefore, in order to keep me from becoming
conceited, I was given a thorn in my flesh,
a messenger of Satan, to torment me. Three times
I pleaded with the Lord to take it away from me.
But he said to me, "My grace is sufficient for you,
for my power is made perfect in weakness."*

2 CORINTHIANS 12:7–9

In his second letter to the Corinthians, the apostle Paul wrote about his thorn in the flesh. We don't know what that misery was specifically—if it was depression, a speech impediment, chronic pain, a spiritual issue of some kind, or something very different. What we do know is that Paul prayed multiple times to be released from this torment. God did respond, but it was with an answer that might have surprised Paul. God said, "My grace is sufficient for you, for my power is made perfect in weakness."

This is a biblical concept that is puzzling, since weakness in a world that values strength seems unacceptable. But God's ways are not our ways, and this truth in tension, as one might call it, is His divine view of our struggles, not ours.

Perhaps we could ask this—what if our weakness forces us to slow down and hear God more clearly? What if that struggle gives us more compassion for others? What if that frailty is made perfect as it illuminates God's power rather than drawing attention to man's efforts? This might help us to understand that thorn—even the one that aches in our own flesh.

*God, when I am weak and afflicted, give me Your
strength. Apart from You I am nothing. Amen. —AH*

A SPECIAL WINDOW OF OPPORTUNITY

Then people brought little children to Jesus for
him to place his hands on them and pray for them.
MATTHEW 19:13

People are very willing to tell you their troubles. Over coffee. Over the fence. Over the counter. Over everything. Friends, family, acquaintances, and even strangers will sometimes tell you the most private details of their ongoing ailments and travails. Rarely will they refuse you if you say you're willing to pray for them during your quiet time with the Lord. This can be a divine appointment that can be a multifaceted opportunity.

Think of the unbeliever and how an offer of prayer might lead the discussion to spiritual matters and then provide an opening to mention the good news of the gospel.

Jesus showed us by example how important it is to intercede for others. Let us pray for ourselves, yes, but let's not neglect the needs of others. A habit of praying for others will cause us to think beyond our own lives, and it will help us lead a more Christ-centered life. The scriptures tell us that the prayer of a righteous person is powerful and effective. What encouragement! What divine assurance!

Who might you pray for right now?

Father, I lift up in prayer the people I have
forgotten in the midst of my own concerns. Grant
me compassion as I seek out those who are hurting
and bring their burdens to You. Amen. —AH

GRANDSTANDING

"But when you pray, go into your room,
close the door and pray to your Father,
who is unseen. Then your Father, who sees
what is done in secret, will reward you."
MATTHEW 6:6

Grandstanding. What a word. It can mean showing off. Yes, we humans are forever trying to impress others and get that spotlight to swivel over to us on that grand stage of life. Even as little tykes we begin the process of learning how to get attention. We wail and wiggle and giggle and coo and shout and sing and sigh and stomp and put our little fists on our hips—anything to be in the limelight and show how important we are. Then we grow up and do adult versions of the same thing.

Bottom line? Humans love attention.

It's safe to say that showing off isn't a deed that is promoted in the Bible. In fact, God says, "But when you pray, go into your room, close the door and pray to your Father, who is unseen. Then your Father, who sees what is done in secret, will reward you."

It's a simple directive. Should be easy, right? It's not that easy. Perhaps we need a prayer to preface our other prayers and ask God to make us prayer warriors who carry the sword of truth rather than the trumpet of pride.

God, help me to remember that when I pray,
I should not be seeking the approval or admiration of
others—I should be seeking You alone. Amen. —AH

THE RECORDINGS
THAT PLAY IN OUR HEADS

Do not put your trust in princes,
in human beings, who cannot save.
PSALM 146:3

If you're human, you've heard the recordings—the ones that play in our heads. Women especially have perfected the art of self-deprecation. You know what I mean—all those cruel remarks that seem to be permanently embedded in our spirits. Such as: You'll never see that dream come true. You'll never amount to anything. You'll never have a family of your own. You're not smart enough, pretty enough, thin enough. God is mad at you. Nobody loves you. You're pathetic.

Sound familiar?

The enemy of our souls would like nothing better than to keep us in a hopeless limbo of either false self-confidence or lack of faith in God. So much so that we can no longer believe the Lord's promises for our lives. Not a good place to be.

Pray that we can have faith in the Lord to empower us to do great things, since the scriptures tell us that we can do all things through Christ who gives us strength. With Him by our sides, we can do all the things we were created to do.

Best advice? Trust God. Delete the recordings!

Lord, it is through You that I find my worth
and value. Shield me from the lies that beat
me down. I am Your child—known, forgiven,
and unconditionally loved. Amen. —AH

BETTER
TO ENDURE

"He cuts off every branch in me that bears no fruit, while every branch that does bear fruit he prunes so that it will be even more fruitful."
JOHN 15:2

Oh, how pleasant to see and smell big blousy roses in full bloom—when they are ripe and full and fragrant. Beautiful. The finest rose-bushes, the strongest and the healthiest specimens, are those which are pruned scrupulously. Ahh, yes, we know where this story illustration is going. No one likes discipline. Not from parents or teachers or police officers or clergymen—or God. It's uncomfortable, and it's embarrassing.

But it's necessary.

How many times have we met children who haven't been disciplined by their parents, who've been given whatever they wanted, whenever they wanted, without any sensitivity to what they really needed? Not a pretty sight. Later, they end up being such miserable adults that they may even miss out on what they were destined to be.

The Lord wants the best for each of us—and the best sometimes requires that uncomfortable d-word. *Discipline.* But wouldn't it be better to endure God's occasional prunings than the devil's persuasions and praise? The Lord wants more for us than we can even imagine for ourselves.

Thank God today for His corrections, for they are full of mercy and love.

They are beautiful.

Dear Lord, thank You for always desiring what is best for me, even if it sometimes requires painful discipline. Amen. —AH

THE
BLACK FLOOD

Out of the depths I cry to you, LORD.
PSALM 130:1

Those black nights. When loneliness becomes like a living thing. When disaster strikes unexpectedly. When you can't seem to draw another breath because the sense of failure or grief or pain seems to consume the very air. The night. The last drop of your hope.

What can you do? Who can you turn to?

God.

He alone is all you need for life and hope on those black nights. He is mighty and powerful and living hope. He is the one who made you, so He knows exactly what you need. Cry out to Him on those black nights. Cling to Him when the world comes crashing in and everyone has fled. When you feel your sin is beyond redemption. When every last drop of hope seems to have dried up. His promises are real. His grace is sufficient. His mercy endures forever. His Word stands. Pray and believe.

He is right here with you. He will never leave you or forsake you. No burden is too great for Him. No sin too dark that He cannot wash it away. He will forgive. He will cradle you in His love. He will reach down and touch your cheek, because He considers you to be His precious child.

Cry out to God.

He is right here.

Heavenly Father, help me to cling to You in times of despair and hopelessness. Wrap me up in the safety of Your arms and soothe me with the peace of Your presence. Amen. —AH

BIG TALK

Then he continued, "Do not be afraid, Daniel.
Since the first day that you set your mind to
gain understanding and to humble yourself
before your God, your words were heard,
and I have come in response to them."
DANIEL 10:12

They say everything is bigger in Texas, but you don't have to live in that big state to experience big pickup trucks. Big hair. Big beef. Big talk. Oww. That last one is as common as mosquitoes in summer and just as welcome. Ever been around someone with BIG talk? When that person Won't. Stop. Talking? It's unnerving. And maddening. After a while your brain goes numb, your eye begins to twitch, and your feet get the itch to run.

There are a lot of people in the world who have this problem. They love the sound of their own voices. They believe their words are a spring of wisdom when they're really a fount of NOISE. Even with a pickax, you couldn't chisel your way into the conversation. You begin to wonder, with so many people talking, is there anybody out there who is listening?

God is.

Yes, your words will be heard. He will respond. That is a promise. What will you say to God?

Lord, thank You for listening to me better than
anyone ever could. When there is a lack of attentive
ears, help me to turn to You instead of despairing.
I have found a friend in You. Amen. —AH

WHEN WE
THINK OF GOD

*For you make me glad by your deeds, Lord; I sing
for joy at what your hands have done. How great
are your works, Lord, how profound your thoughts!*
PSALM 92:4–5

Do you ever feel the flatness of life—as if you were one of those cartoon characters who's been bopped on the head with a mallet and your head now meets your knees? Do you approach the day with words like these: *One-dimensional. Dull. Gray. Dreary. Stale. Tedious. Humdrum.*

The God of the universe wants us to start our day with a different mindset. There is nothing about God and His creation that is humdrum. Nothing. He made the elegant silhouette of a swan. The shimmer of a sunrise on a pristine glacier. The whispers of tropical wildlife still unknown to man.

When we think of God and His creation, our words should be transformed. They might become: *Mysterious. Exotic. Breathtaking. Radiant. Exhilarating. Invigorating. Miraculous.* Prayer is connecting with that mind. That heart. That brilliance. That life and color. That perfection.

Let us come into His presence with thanksgiving and praise. Let us come to know Him who is extraordinary beyond compare. And through that communion, let us see His world and His people as they were meant to be.

*Creator God, open my eyes to the richness
and vibrancy of life. I want to encounter each
day with the freedom and joy that is abundant
in a relationship with You. Amen.* —AH

LIVING IN
THE SHADOWS

*"Who can hide in secret places so that I
cannot see them?" declares the LORD. "Do not
I fill heaven and earth?" declares the LORD.*

JEREMIAH 23:24

Evil lurks in shrouded places, the murky crevices of life. It hates the light. So sin tries to conceal itself.

We might think we're hiding our secret little sins from God, but there is no such thing as secrets from God. He sees all. And to believe that some sins are small is a lie we create to make ourselves feel better. Hiding from God? It is the dream that we wouldn't want to come true.

Still, though, we try to live in the shadows. Fearful of stepping into the light of heaven—His light. Because once bathed in His divine illumination, we can never see sin the same way again. As something livable. Doable. Acceptable. In that light we see that we are naked, just as Adam and Eve did after their disobedience. We see what must be changed. Our hearts. Our minds. All of our being. In that holy light we see love in a new way. We long for goodness. We desire to be clothed in righteousness. We can see our way to heaven.

Let us step out of the dark corners of sin and into the light of Christ, where we can confess our sins and accept His love and forgiveness. Where eternal life will be ours.

*Savior God, give me the strength to step into
Your holy, cleansing light. Amen.* —AH

PRAYING
THE SCRIPTURES

*All Scripture is God-breathed and is
useful for teaching, rebuking, correcting
and training in righteousness.*
2 Timothy 3:16

Have you ever needed a little help with your prayers? You wanted to say more that was on your heart, but you couldn't quite put it into words? Since the entire Bible is God-breathed, and it is valuable in many ways, using the scriptures to help you to pray is a wonderful way to speak the truth and get right to the heart of what you're trying to say.

Here's an example from Psalm 103:1–5. In this passage, the second person reference has simply been changed to first person. But to repeat the Psalms or any other scripture in this way is not to be thought of or used as a chant as some people do in other religions. Nor are we to think that there is supernatural power in the words themselves, for it is God who is all-powerful and who hears and responds to our petitions.

Try infusing your prayers with a helping from God's holy Word.

*Praise the Lord, my soul; all my inmost being, praise his
holy name. Praise the Lord, my soul, and forget not all his
benefits—who forgives all my sins and heals all my diseases,
who redeems my life from the pit and crowns me with love and
compassion, who satisfies my desires with good things so that
my youth is renewed like the eagle's.*

*Lord, infuse my prayers with passion,
sincerity, and praise. May our communion
be beautiful and strong. Amen. —AH*

EXPECT
A MIRACLE

You turned my wailing into dancing;
you removed my sackcloth and clothed me with joy.
PSALM 30:11

How do you rise up from your prayer time with the Lord? Be honest. As if nothing will really happen? As if your words have flowed from your heart and will spill into nothingness? Or perhaps you go away from your prayers with enthusiasm and heartfelt faith, but by the afternoon you are weary and disheartened again. In a world that doesn't believe in the supernatural, it is easy to make assumptions that a miracle is impossible. That miracles only happened in biblical times. Or the assumption that miracles seem to be for everyone—but you.

And yet that is not the truth.

God does hear our prayers. He does listen. He will respond. He already knows our every need. Know that in His timing, our tears will turn to joy. That our hobbling, stumbling, pain-filled steps will turn to dancing. It will be in His way, His timing. Don't struggle in this truth, but rest in its beauty. The Lord's timing is perfect, and His answers are full of mercy and justice and love.

Pray.

Expect a miracle.

Keep the faith.

Sovereign God, forgive my unbelief and give
me great faith. Help me to trust in Your plans
and remember that in all things, You work for
the good of those who love You. Amen. —AH

SPA DAY
FOR THE SOUL

*One of those days Jesus went
out to a mountainside to pray, and
spent the night praying to God.*
LUKE 6:12

We women enjoy going to the spa—relaxing with a hot stone massage or getting our toenails painted the color of red-hot candies. Or indulging in a facial that sends us into orbital bliss. Gotta love it, eh?

We like to spoil our bodies in every way. But what about pampering our spirits? We tend to neglect what can't be seen, and yet we are made of spirit as well as flesh. So, what about having a spa day for the soul? Talk about rejuvenating. We would come away with a new outlook, a smile on our lips and a song in our hearts. Our spirits might even feel ten years younger.

When Jesus walked among us, He showed us how important prayer was. It says in God's Word that Christ went out to the mountainside to pray and spent the night praying to God. He knew how powerful and vital prayer was and how He needed it to stay the course.

So, are you ready to schedule a spa day for your soul? A day of prayer and communion with your Lord? Or even an hour on Sunday? The luxury of this refreshment is gratis, and its beautification will be a lift to the body and spirit.

*Lord, help me to remember to regularly refresh
my spirit through prayer. My soul needs You as
much as my body needs oxygen. Amen. —AH*

WAY OFF-BALANCE

*"I have come that they may have
life, and have it to the full."*
JOHN 10:10

We've all heard the racket that a washing machine can make when it goes off-balance in the spin cycle. It's a *kabang, kabang, kabang* that will either drive you nuts or make you sprint into the laundry room to shift the contents around in hopes of a smoother ride for your clothes—and for your brain. Don't some days or even whole weeks seem to have that same off-balanced *kabang*? You know what I mean? People say ugly things. Your family and friends misunderstand you even though you meant well. Your boss treats you a little lower than the dust. Your body seems to be falling apart. You find yourself in a heap of trouble, and you have no idea how to make things right.

We desperately want to sprint into some celestial laundry room to fix the load. To put everything back in balance, so our lives—as well as our pounding heads—will stop with that infernal kabanging. Yet we can do nothing on our own.

God made the universe, and so He is the only one who can fix this sin-riddled, off-balanced planet of ours.

When Jesus came to earth, He willingly gave up His life as atonement for our sins. Jesus is the world's stability, and that beautiful balance, that full life, that quiet rest, is only a prayer away.

*Jesus, please give me the stability and
peace that can only come from You. I place
my life in Your hands. Amen. —AH*

THE HARDEST PRAYER

*Going a little farther, he fell with his face
to the ground and prayed, "My Father,
if it is possible, may this cup be taken from
me. Yet not as I will, but as you will."*

MATTHEW 26:39

When we pray, asking God for help, we have a good idea of what we want. We might even think, *This is my life. I'm the one living it, and I know exactly what I need.*

Yet we don't. We can't possibly know. We are human and more than a little fallible. Only God knows exactly what we need. So, when we pray, we should end our petitions with "Your will be done." Hmmm. We've got to put a bit of thought into that part of the prayer. It means we'd have to trust God for our every need. All the time. Night and day. Uh-oh. Do we really trust Him that much?

Even Jesus, on the night before His crucifixion, when He knew He would be betrayed by His followers and die a brutal death on the cross, Jesus still ended His prayer with—"Your will be done." Yes, Jesus did ask God for a way out—in other words, was there another way for redemption to come to man other than His death on the cross? In fact, Christ asked God this question three times. But in the end, our Lord said the words "Your will be done."

Jesus trusted. And so should we.

*God, even when I am discouraged and
afraid, help me to trust in Your will for my
life. You know what's best. Amen.* —AH

NO OTHER NAME

For this reason I kneel before the Father, from whom
every family in heaven and on earth derives its name.
EPHESIANS 3:14–15

Some family names are problematic. Perhaps they resemble the people they represent a little too closely (the Stouts, who are just a wee bit on the heavy side), or perhaps the name doesn't seem to fit at all (the Loves, who are not loving at all). Or perhaps the family name is fine alone, but then becomes a problem when joined with another (Mrs. Mary Stout-Bottom might want to rethink that hyphen).

Here in his letter to the Ephesians, Paul is referring to the fact that every family (in Greek, *patria*) comes from the Father (in Greek, *pater*). We are one, down to our roots, even our root word. As Paul goes on to describe, we are "rooted and established in love" (v.17). So whether the knee that kneels before the Father is Gentile or Jew; black, white, brown, or some color in between; clothed in rich silk or showing through shredded denim—no matter where your family line has now ended up or what convoluted path it took to get here, no matter what, you can now come freely before the God in heaven and call Him Father.

And maybe in prayer, every family can set aside prejudices and fears and for a moment grasp "how wide and long and high and deep is the love of Christ" (v. 18).

Father God, teach me how to love
like You. Amen. —ML

MEET, PRAY, LOVE

*Dear children, let us not love with words
or speech but with actions and in truth.*
1 JOHN 3:18

This verse is often used to lecture Christians today who are happy to sit in pews and on chairs and listen to sermons about love and generosity, yet go out into the streets and refuse to give a homeless man a hand. It is true. You cannot just pray for people and then, when faced with a real, live, breathing person in front of your face, refuse to do them some good. You must act, for as James famously penned, "Faith by itself, if it is not accompanied by action, is dead" (James 2:17).

Sometimes it is also true that that action involves words and speech. You can love someone through prayer. At times the most loving thing you can do for a person is pray with them and for them. When a person is deep in grief, holding their hands and praying with them for comfort is worth a whole shop full of flowers. When a person is stuck in depression, seeking them out and thanking God for them can be better than any other act. When a person is anxious, a walk out in the fresh air with a friend and a request to God for calm and assurance can be just exactly what the doctor ordered.

Love with actions. But love with words and speech too. And do all of it in truth.

*Dear God, help me to have courage
to pray with others. Amen. —ML*

TONGUE TWISTER

Now you must also rid yourselves of all
such things as these: anger, rage, malice,
slander, and filthy language from your lips.
COLOSSIANS 3:8

Perhaps there are people who can pray with profanity, but that would be a peculiar possibility. It would be akin to sending stinky bouquets or mailing love letters laced with lies.

No, going to God is likely to have the same effect on a person's tongue as sitting in a pew with a priest or realizing a child is in earshot. We all try to put on our Sunday-best speech when praying.

So, if you happen to be a person who has some trouble controlling your tongue, you might try this exercise: Every time you want to swear, or spew angry insults, or call someone names, pray instead. Pray for self-control. Pray for patience. Pray for kindness. Pray for courtesy. Pray for respect. Pray for a better heart. Pray for more grace. Pray for the people you are angry with. Pray for the project that is causing you to curse. Pray for the coworker who gets on your last nerve. Pray for the ones who have hurt you. Pray for God's vengeance and not your own.

Pray for a new vocabulary.

Dear Lord, please make me tongue-tied
at just the right times. Amen. —ML

CONFIDENCE

*Let us then approach God's throne of grace
with confidence, so that we may receive mercy
and find grace to help us in our time of need.*
HEBREWS 4:16

Do you have a robe-and-slippers friend? Someone who could just show up at your door on a Saturday morning, and you'd be in your robe and slippers, and she wouldn't care? It's a wonderful thing to have a friend so close, you know you could approach her at any time of day, in any state, and no matter what, she'd make time for you.

It is an even more wonderful thing to know that our God, the King of kings and Lord of lords, allows us—invites us—to approach His throne with confidence. He tells us to have confidence for two reasons. The first is that He understands. He has experienced everything we have, and more. He knows what it is like to be us—He has felt the weakness of the human form and the vulnerability of the human heart. The second reason is that He overcomes. He has experienced all of this and yet not succumbed to the sinful will. He was obedient, even to death.

So this is our God. He understands and overcomes and lives today. He invites us to come to Him fully trusting that He will accept us as we are.

Even in our robe and slippers.

*Lord God, I bow in awe of Your grace and mercy.
Let me learn how to live for You. Amen. —ML*

AN OFFERING

*May my prayer be set before you
like incense; may the lifting up of my
hands be like the evening sacrifice.*
PSALM 141:2

It is not entirely clear exactly why or when the custom of burning incense as a part of religious practices came to be. Perhaps it was a way to mask the odor of the dead animals killed and burned as sacrifices to God. Perhaps it was a way to both literally and figuratively clear the air between the people and God. Or perhaps it was just that people like nice-smelling things.

For whatever reason, the burning of incense continues to this day to be an important part of many religious services. It is an expression of something from us going up to heaven. An aromatic love letter to God.

The offerings of old given to God had to be pure, clean, and whole. So we should try to come before God either in that form or ready to submit to Him making us so.

"May my prayer be. . .like incense"—strong and sweet words, full of life. "May the lifting up of my hands be like the evening sacrifice"—empty of self and wholly devoted to the will of the Lord.

Lord, make me a living sacrifice. Amen. —ML

CALL TO ME

*"Call to me and I will answer you and tell you
great and unsearchable things you do not know."*
JEREMIAH 33:3

The word *unsearchable* seems a near impossibility in today's technological age. Is there anything that Google cannot search for? Apparently so.

God tells us to call to Him and He will answer. That arrangement alone is a miracle in itself—that the Lord of the universe would even want us to speak to Him. But even more amazing is the idea that God would let us in on His secrets—that He would take the time and effort to be our teacher.

This relationship with God, this closeness, is reflected again and again in scripture. It's there in Abraham staring at the stars, it's there in Moses on the mountain, and it's there in Mary's womb. God wants us to know, to be certain of the fact that He is with us, in us, through us.

God wants more from us than a Q and A session. He wants a constant conversation. He wants more than what we might "ask Siri." He wants to know the deepest questions of our souls—the ones that keep us up at night or frighten us with their proportions.

Oswald Chambers said in *My Utmost for His Highest*, "We look upon prayer as a means of getting things for ourselves; the Bible's idea of prayer is that we may get to know God Himself."

*Dear Lord, thank You for the chance
to know You more. Amen. —ML*

ANYTHING

*"You may ask me for anything in
my name, and I will do it."*
JOHN 14:14

Anything. Ask *anything*. That's what Jesus said. And Jesus doesn't lie.

Humans are funny creatures. God gave us the gift of speech and we just can't seem to stop getting tripped up on words. The God who knows every tongue is not so concerned with words—His concern is meanings.

So Jesus says "ask anything," and visions of cars, houses, and perfect hair pop into our heads. But the sentences before and after help us to understand the meaning. "I will do whatever you ask in my name, so that the Father may be glorified in the Son" (v. 13). The point of the "whatever" here is that it needs to be something that would bring glory to God. How do you do that? Read this verse: "If you love me, keep my commands" (v. 15). By being obedient to Jesus, we will do what is needed to love God and love others—bringing glory to God in the process (and not to ourselves).

If we are busy keeping Jesus' commands and thinking about glorifying God, there's a good chance we won't ask for just "anything." We'll ask for what we need to fulfill those commands. We'll ask for what we need to glorify God. Peace. Faith. Grace. Mercy. Love. Courage. We'll ask for the things that count.

Anything.

*Dear Father, help me know what
to ask for. Amen. —ML*

WITH AUTHORITY

*"Therefore I tell you, whatever you ask for in prayer,
believe that you have received it, and it will be yours."*
MARK 11:24

The scene in Mark 11 brings to mind any stereotypical mob boss out for a stroll. If the big guy doesn't get what he wants, he just "takes care" of things. Ba-da-bing, ba-da-boom, no more problems.

Jesus was hungry. And apparently, a little grumpy. He spies a fig tree with leaves on it—but no figs. What gives? (Never mind that it wasn't fig season. A good tree bears fruit, right?) So Jesus curses the tree.

His fellas hear all this, but no one's gonna be a tree hugger. They continue on their way to Jerusalem, where Jesus goes into one of the most glorious rages ever described in the Bible. (Told you He was grumpy.) He literally puts the fear of God into the rival gang (the chief priests and teachers of the law).

The guys are walking back home from all this excitement when they come upon a black, gnarled stump of a tree—the fig tree, withered right down to its roots. Jesus tells them that if they believe what they say will happen in prayer, it will be done.

Who could have questioned Him? No one. And that's the point of Mark 11.

Jesus was not just another teacher or nice guy. Jesus was God. When God says your prayers will make things happen, you better believe Him.

*God, help me make things happen
for Your kingdom. Amen. —ML*

LADY PERSISTENCE

"Will not God bring about justice for his chosen ones, who cry out to him day and night?"
LUKE 18:7

Sometimes—admit it—you feel like giving up. You have a chronic illness that just never seems to get any better. You have a workload that never lets up. You have some family struggle that just cannot be resolved, no matter how hard you try.

Keep praying.

You keep trying to learn a new thing, but your grades don't show your effort. You want a relationship to work, but you don't know what to do. You keep looking for a job, but no one seems to be hiring.

Keep praying.

Jesus painted the picture for us of a widow bringing a complaint before a judge. She wanted justice. The uncaring judge wanted to be left alone. But the widow kept coming, no matter how many times he refused her. Finally, he gave in and actually did the right thing.

Jesus pointed out that if unjust judges here on earth can decide cases to bring about justice, then God certainly can and will do the same for His children. He won't keep putting them off. He will always see that justice gets done.

Dear judge of all, please help to bring justice and peace to the situation on my mind. Amen. —ML

REFRESH

"Repent, then, and turn to God, so that
your sins may be wiped out, that times of
refreshing may come from the Lord."
Acts 3:19

Surely one of the prayers most often prayed is "God, I'm sorry." It must be right up there with "God, help!"

Prayer is a profound and essential part of repentance. You cannot repent without coming before God. In our present time, you cannot come before God without prayer.

Certainly it's not anyone's favorite prayer to say. To come before the Holy One and declare the ways in which you have been most definitely not holy is uncomfortable, to say the least. For some the encounter could even be sickening.

You cannot get rid of a wound without exposing it and cleaning it out. You cannot repent and start to heal without exposing your heart to God.

Let God wipe away your sins. Let God forgive you, so you can know how to forgive others. Start over. Start fresh.

Then don't take the same steps when you walk away. Try something new. Walk a different way. Set up a new routine. Make sure prayer is part of your daily schedule. Not just one part. Let prayer prepare you for your day, let prayer be a time of rest throughout your day, and let prayer end your day with thanksgiving. If you do this, the times of refreshing will come.

Dear Lord, refresh my spirit and
renew my heart. Amen. —ML

LIKE AN EAGLE

Like an eagle that stirs up its nest and hovers
over its young. . . . The LORD alone led him.
DEUTERONOMY 32:11–12

It is good to remember the kind of person we are addressing when we pray. God is mighty like the ocean and strong like the wind. God is unending like the sky and enduring like the mountains. God is peaceful like a quiet sea and patient like shore rocks that take the waves. God is all-powerful, all-knowing, always with us.

God is big and unsearchable in many ways. Yet He lets us know Him and learn about Him. God is a whispering voice in our souls, and yet His Word shouts truth.

God is huge and grand and impossible to fathom. He is our Father—deliverer of justice, ruler of peace, rescuer and redeemer.

God is like the eagle, which nurtures its eggs, turning them over at just the right time and keeping them at just the right temperature for proper growth. God is like the eagle, which protects its young chicks, covering them with its wings. God is like the eagle, playing with its young, letting them take chances and then always being there to catch them when they fall.

God is like the eagle, teaching us to fly and carrying us high over the hard parts.

This is the God we call on when we pray.

Dear God, thank You for Your tender,
caring love. Amen. —ML

NEAR

*What other nation is so great as to have
their gods near them the way the LORD our
God is near us whenever we pray to him?*

DEUTERONOMY 4:7

Moses makes a rather undeniable point in his speech to the Israelites. He reminds them what God has done for them and the way in which God has spoken to them. He reminds them of these things as a warning to them not to try to make a form to fit God—not to worship idols of their own making.

Look around at the people who were living at the time and it's not hard to see why this warning was needed. Many people worshipped other gods, often linked with the seasons or natural elements. Every god they had had a form. It was common for people to create shapes and pictures and statues to represent their gods. People like to have something to hold on to—a way of understanding something that they can't understand.

Moses reminds the people that they need not do that. They don't have to paint a picture or shape a statue. God is right there with them. They can know Him by His voice, by His commands He has given them, and by the promises He made to them. They can be sure of Him by remembering all He has done for them and telling these stories to the next generation, so they remember too.

God is near. No other god comes close.

Dear God, thank You for coming near. Amen. —ML

WAITING
FOR MERCY

But you, dear friends, by. . .praying in the
Holy Spirit, keep yourselves in God's love
as you wait for the mercy of our Lord Jesus
Christ to bring you to eternal life.
JUDE 20–21

Some people actively long for heaven. For various reasons, they are finished with this world and ready to move on to the next.

Jude reminds you that you must keep growing in the knowledge and love of God, even when you are done with the ways of this world. You must keep "building yourselves up in your most holy faith" (v. 20). You must keep reading God's Word, studying its meaning, and living a life of service and obedience and hope.

You must keep "praying in the Holy Spirit." You must regularly go to God in prayer, spending time listening to what He has for you and laying your requests before Him. You must let God search your mind and heart and discover any wrong thinking or wrongdoing in you. You must continue to ask forgiveness for your sins.

By doing these things, you will keep "in God's love as you wait for the mercy of our Lord Jesus Christ to bring you to eternal life."

You may be done with this world, but God is not done with you. Wait for God's mercy, but don't wait in idleness. Wait and hope and pray.

Dear Lord Jesus, we long to live with You.
Please come soon. Amen. —ML

A PRAYER FOR PASTORS

Pray also for me, that whenever I speak, words may be given me so that I will fearlessly make known the mystery of the gospel.
EPHESIANS 6:19

How often do you pray for pastors? Pastors may be paid or not, but they are people who devote the majority of their lives to the teaching, development, care, counseling, and nurturing of God's flock. They serve in one of the hardest and most stressful jobs a person can have. Why? Because their job 100 percent of the time is dealing with people—and most often people in some kind of physical, spiritual, mental, or emotional need.

So pray for your pastors. Pray that they be able to endure long nights and long phone calls. Pray that they have time to study and be refreshed. Pray that they have clear understanding of God's Word and ability to speak truth well.

Pray for courage. Pray that they will not be afraid to stop someone from a life of destruction. Pray that they will be confident in God's love for them. Pray they will be strong in fighting off temptation.

Pray for wisdom. Pray that they will be able to pick their battles. Pray that they will know when to be silent. Pray that their understanding of people will be strengthened by experience and by prayer.

Pray for an unending well of energy. Pray for the ability to share unconditional love. Pray for an eternal life with God.

Pray for your pastors.

Dear God, thank You for Your servants. Please help me to build them up. Amen. —ML

INNER
THOUGHTS

For who knows a person's thoughts
except their own spirit within them?
1 CORINTHIANS 2:11

Where do your thoughts roam in the space of one day?

From wondering what to cook for supper, to thinking about your own queasy stomach, to dwelling on what disease you might have, to getting distracted with that cute video of the singing kitten, to remembering the dog needs its shots, to wishing you didn't have so many things on your to-do list, to being frustrated over the state of your house, to being frustrated over the state of your country, to listening to the news, to listening to your friend and wondering why she gets herself in such messes, to wondering about your own messes—the list could go on and on, couldn't it?

That's just one normal day. Or maybe ten minutes.

No matter how close you are to someone, it's impossible to know their thoughts all the time. Yet the spirit within us knows. And the Spirit of God knows the thoughts of God. So with that Spirit given to us by God, when we pray and ask, we can know a little about what God wants for us. That Spirit prays for us when we have no words, laying our thoughts before God. It's frightening and wonderful all at the same time.

Kind of like your thoughts.

Dear God, help me to guard my
thoughts from evil. Amen. —ML

ALL
DAY LONG

Guide me in your truth and teach me, for you are
God my Savior, and my hope is in you all day long.
PSALM 25:5

There was once a popular candy that people called an all-day sucker. The reason it had this name, of course, is that it was such a big lollipop, it was supposed to last through a kid's licks all day long.

Let's face it. That's a lot to ask of a sucker. Most kids are content to lick a little, but at some point the urge to crunch and consume that candy conquers all. *Crunch, crunch*—and it's gone. It would be surprising if it lasted past lunchtime, much less all day.

Sometimes our focus on God doesn't make it that long either. But it is such a relief to know that God is infinitely more durable than an all-day sucker, and He is always available to us. Whether we take a day and just reflect on Him the entire day, or whether our thoughts flit back and forth between earthly concerns and more spiritual matters, God is always ready to listen to us.

There is no time when it is not appropriate to call on Him. Unlike the all-day sucker, which might get frowned upon at formal gatherings, God's truth is always applicable. Every occasion can be a time to learn something about and lean on God. All we have to do is ask, and He will guide us.

Dear God, I place my hope in You. Amen. —ML

SON THOUGH HE WAS

He offered up prayers and petitions with fervent cries and tears to the one who could save him from death.
HEBREWS 5:7

There's an amazing description of Jesus in Hebrews 5.

Jesus walked on this earth with us. He was born and died, like we are born and will die. He suffered more than we could ever know. Just as there come days when we lift up desperate prayers to God through tears, Jesus prayed and cried too. Just as we sometimes have to face hard things and are not given an easy out, Jesus didn't get the easy way out either. He prayed and asked, "God please, if. . ." But He did not get the "if." He got the "Thy will be done" part instead.

Son though He was, His burdens were not taken away.

Son though He was, He was not rescued in a daring last-minute escape.

Son though He was, He did not triumph over His captors. At least, not that time.

Instead, "Son though he was, he learned obedience from what he suffered" and then, when He had fulfilled the prophecies and conquered death, He "became the source of eternal salvation for all who obey him" (vv. 8–9).

Why should we expect answers to our prayers to be different from His—Son that He is?

Dear God, help me to accept Your will. Amen. —ML

PRAYER OF A RIGHTEOUS PERSON

Therefore confess your sins to each other and
pray for each other so that you may be healed.
JAMES 5:16

James is a clear, practical writer. In chapter 5 of his message, James tells the hearers when to pray. "Is anyone among you in trouble?" Pray. "Is anyone happy?" Praise God. "Is anyone among you sick?" Gather your church elders and let them pray over you (vv. 13–14).

He gives you the results with complete confidence as well. "And the prayer offered in faith will make the sick person well; the Lord will raise them up. If they have sinned, they will be forgiven" (v. 15). He urges people to pray for each other so they can receive healing, for "the prayer of a righteous person is powerful and effective" (v.16).

Why is the prayer of righteous people so powerful and effective? There are at least three reasons: 1) the faith they have; 2) the faith people have in them; 3) the faith they don't have yet. A righteous person is a faithful person—a person who knows God, and whose hope is consistently settled on God. When they pray, God knows they mean it. The people who hear them know it too. They see the righteous person's life and who their hope is in, and this strengthens their faith.

Lastly, the prayer of the righteous is powerful because of what they lack. God's strength shines in their weakness.

Dear Lord, thank You for righteous people
who trust in You. Amen. —ML

FRIEND AND INTERCESSOR

*"My intercessor is my friend as
my eyes pour out tears to God."*
JOB 16:20

Job was a man in need of a true friend. You have probably heard about the suffering of Job. (If you haven't, read the first couple of chapters of the book of Job—but be prepared for a shock.) The story of Job is about a man full of grief and hurt, a man allowed by God to be tested. He was surrounded by so-called friends, who perhaps meant well, but whose words weren't exactly helpful. About them Job said, "You are miserable comforters, all of you!" (v. 2), and he was right.

We have a better friend and comforter than any person we could find on earth. We have Jesus. Jesus is always there for us. Jesus speaks to God on our behalf. Can we imagine a better person to stand up for us? Jesus "pleads with God as one pleads for a friend" (v. 21).

And what does He plead? When we repent of our sins, He pleads for our forgiveness. When we have been hurt, He pleads for our restoration. When we stand before God to be judged for our worth, He stands in for us and says, "I make this one worthy."

It is good to have friends in high places. It's better still to have a friend willing to bring us up with Him.

*Dear Jesus, thank You for pleading
for me. Amen.* —ML

BEST FRIENDS

*Restore us, O God; make your
face shine on us, that we may be saved.*
PSALM 80:3

If you've ever had a best friend, you may know the pleasure and joy that comes when meeting together after a long separation. You may not see each other for years and years, yet when you speak, it is as if the years all fall away and the connections are still all there, firing away as if you'd never let the engine cool.

True friends connect on deeper levels than what can be affected by time and circumstances. They care about each other's thoughts and feelings, not just each other's comings and goings. They know all the essential bits that make up a person's character—the history that defines a person as well as the goals that drive a person.

A true friend can be someone you have known from a young age or someone you met later in life. It may be someone you've gone through a struggle with or someone who helped you out of a troubling time. No matter what happens, that person is able to love you unconditionally.

God is your best friend. Whether you know Him now or not, whether you've loved Him since childhood or only since yesterday—anytime you sit with Him and pray to Him, it can be as though you've just joined a conversation that has been going on forever. A conversation that can go on forever still.

*Dear God, remind me You are always
there for me. Amen. —ML*

DOXOLOGY

*By day the LORD directs his love, at night his song
is with me—a prayer to the God of my life.*
PSALM 42:8

Have you ever prayed in song? Over and over, the psalmists prayed in the form of songs sung to God. These might be songs meant to be sung on your own or songs to be sung with a group of people. In either case, the words of the songs are meant to do the same things as spoken prayer—to focus our thoughts on God, to give Him praise, and to lay before Him our desires.

There are a plethora of songs today you could choose to sing as prayers to God. If your prayer life is ever feeling a little stagnant, try singing a prayer instead of speaking one. The best thing is you don't even have to be a good singer—just make sure no one's around to hear you! Or in fact, let them hear you anyway. If they are not blessed by the words of your prayer, they will be blessed by the comic relief.

Praise God from whom all blessings flow;
Praise Him, all creatures here below;
Praise Him above, ye heavenly host;
Praise Father, Son, and Holy Ghost.
(Thomas Ken, 1637–1711)

Dear God, thank You for the gift of song.
May my praise be music to Your ears. Amen. —ML

MY SOUL TO KEEP

*"Let the little children come to me,
and do not hinder them, for the kingdom
of God belongs to such as these."*
MARK 10:14

Some of the best prayers you will ever hear may come from the lips of a child. Children speak to God as if they were speaking to their teacher or their grandpa or their dog Fido. They use the words that come naturally to them and don't try to sound fancy or serious.

Children innocently reveal all their secrets and sometimes the secrets of others. They come clean about every size of mistake or wrong they ever did or that was ever done to them or by somebody nearby them. They empty their little souls of all their burdens. Perhaps that's what makes them so bouncy.

Children will pray prayers about the ridiculous and the sublime all at the same time, sometimes even in the same breath. They have no boundaries between them and their Father, no walls to break down, no veils to hide behind.

It is no wonder that Jesus asked for the little children to be allowed to come to Him. How refreshing it must be for God to hear the prayers of hearts and minds that have not yet been made world-weary. We might do well to shed our grown-up manners once in a while and pray with the children: "Now I lay me down to sleep, I pray the Lord my soul to keep."

*Dear Father, remind me that I am
Your child still. Amen.* —ML

TEMPLE PRAYERS

*Don't you know that you yourselves are God's
temple and that God's Spirit dwells in your midst?*
1 CORINTHIANS 3:16

A lesson on the geography of God: God is where you are. You are where God is. You don't have to go to a special place to pray to God. You don't have to have an altar. You don't have to be in the high places. You don't have to be in a valley. You don't have to go to a church, a cathedral, a temple, or a synagogue.

As Paul told the Corinthians, you—not you by yourself, but the collective you—are the temple. We as the body of Christ are the gathering place where people can meet God. God's Spirit dwells among us, among the whole family of us. Not in one special person or exclusive place.

So when you want to pray, pray. Pray where you are, wherever that may be. In your car, on the street, in the woods, in your laundry room. Treat that time as set apart to God in your mind, though it is not physically set apart by a sign or walls or doors.

Be on the lookout for those who seek to destroy God's temple by setting up rules and regulations that God Himself never made. When you want to pray, pray. Wherever you are, wherever you go, whenever you happen to think of speaking to God. Your temple prayers can happen anywhere.

*Help me, God, to protect Your temple—
the body of believers. Amen. —ML*

HOLLOW

*See to it that no one takes you captive
through hollow and deceptive philosophy.*
COLOSSIANS 2:8

Perhaps more than ever, there is a jungle of ideas out there in the world, and all are easily accessible through the internet, on the television, on the radio, and even shouting from billboards. Many of these messages are hollow—they are full of pictures and colorful presentations, captivating in their entertainment value, but lacking substance.

Yet these messages can easily distract from the truth.

The best way to guard against this distraction and the temptation to become entangled in ungodly thinking is to immerse yourself in God's Word. You can do this by reading the Bible, of course. Yet you can also do this through prayer. In prayer, you have direct access to the plan and will of God. Though God may not speak to you through a burning bush or give you tablets of stone, through consistent submission of your will to His and through the daily disciplines of faith, you can become familiar with the thoughts and reasons and plans He has for living in His kingdom—and for your particular path.

Don't let your mind be filled with fluff and cloudy thinking. Put your trust in God and let Him fill you up.

*Dear God, help me to be able to discern
what is true and what is not. Amen.* —ML

BLESSING

"The LORD bless you and keep you."
NUMBERS 6:24

Sometimes the simplest prayers are the ones that make a difference.

This particular blessing of the Israelites from Numbers 6 has been quoted countless times—in weddings and funerals, as toasts at dinners, as memory verses for children, and so on. People have heard it so many times, in fact, that they probably don't even recognize it as a prayer anymore, and chances are that they don't have the faintest idea where it is from.

Yet this simple prayer has given comfort and peace to many hearts. It has put smiles on people's faces and made busy people stop for a moment to listen and hear the word of the Lord (even if they didn't realize it).

The Lord first gave this prayer to Moses to tell Aaron and his sons, the priests of Israel, how to bless the Israelites. After telling him the words to say, God says that this is the way the priests will "put my name on the Israelites" (v. 27). It was like a tag on the people saying "This nation belongs to God."

There's a lot of strength and goodness in repetition—especially in a reminder of who God is and who we are to Him.

"The LORD make his face shine on you and be gracious to you; the LORD turn his face toward you and give you peace" (vv. 25–26).

Lord, thank You for prayers that span
generations. Amen. —ML

PRAYING FOR
THE PERSECUTORS

Bless those who persecute you; bless and do not curse.
ROMANS 12:14

If you've ever been the target of ridicule, ever been bullied or humiliated, or ever been hurt by someone simply for what you believe, you may find Paul's instruction to be difficult to swallow.

It's all well and good to say "bless your enemies," but how do you actually do that? Are you supposed to bring them gifts? Do you take them dinner? Should you subject yourself to weekly beatings?

Possibly. (Well, not that last one.) You can find more clues about how this actually works in the surrounding words. "Be devoted to one another in love. Honor one another above yourselves. Never be lacking in zeal, but keep your spiritual fervor, serving the Lord. Be joyful in hope, patient in affliction, faithful in prayer. Share with the Lord's people who are in need. Practice hospitality. . . . Rejoice with those who rejoice; mourn with those who mourn" (vv. 10–13,15).

You are to act toward your persecutors as you should to those you love: honoring them above yourself, serving them, sharing with them. Rejoice with them when good things happen, and mourn with them when bad times come their way. Show them how you find joy in hope and how you bear the suffering they inflict on you, and pray for them faithfully, asking God to soften their hearts and to help you find a way to love them.

Dear Lord, give me words to pray for those who have hurt me, and help me to mean them. Amen. —ML

OPEN
YOUR EYES

I pray that the eyes of your heart may
be enlightened in order that you may know
the hope to which he has called you.

EPHESIANS 1:18

Do you know someone who needs to open her eyes? Some people keep their eyes shut tight to the world, trying to hide from their fears. Some people are filled with greed and shut their eyes to avoid seeing poverty and need. Some are burdened with guilt—they just can't face the person in the mirror.

Maybe you are one of these people. God does not want you to live a life blinded by the past. He wants you to live a life grounded in and aimed at the hope to which He has called us all.

That hope is not like anything else you have to hope for in this world. It's not a vague wish for better days. It's not the hope for happiness or for a nice house and a good job. It is the "riches of his glorious inheritance in his holy people, and his incomparably great power for us who believe" (vv. 18–19). The same power that raised Christ from the dead is the power that we have access to. The same inheritance that will be shared by all the great biblical heroes of old and the modern-day saints can be ours too.

Ask God to help you keep your eyes wide open. The view is beautiful—don't miss it!

Dear Lord, open my eyes wide and help
me to enlighten others. Amen. —ML

QUENCHABLE

"In your anger do not sin."
EPHESIANS 4:26

It's no wonder so many words that describe anger have to do with fire. Anger can flare up as quickly as a single spark in a dry hayfield. It takes only seconds for it to exploit some weakness, to consume some fuel to feed its flames. But a well-built fire can smolder for hours and even days after it has died down. Unless it is completely demolished and the fuel spread out, the fire could start up again at the first touch of a dry twig or a warm breeze.

If you know you have a temper (or even if you're sure you don't), the one way to grow stronger in restraining your anger is to pray regularly. Pray for self-control and patience. Pray for understanding and perspective, so you can stop minor irritations from growing into something harder to tame. Pray for the simple ability to just keep your mouth shut. Start with physical control, then work up to calming your thoughts and emotions. Ask God to remind you to use anger management strategies—to walk away, to breathe deeply, to count to ten.

Pray hard. Do whatever it takes to keep your anger from becoming a fire you cannot control—to keep it from hurting others or yourself. Ask God for forgiveness when you mess up, and ask Him to teach you to forgive others.

Don't let a spark destroy your whole household.

*Dear God, help me to control my mind
and my mouth. Amen.* —ML

WHATEVER

*Whatever happens, conduct yourselves
in a manner worthy of the gospel of Christ.*
PHILIPPIANS 1:27

The washer dies midcycle. The cat throws up right before company comes over. Nobody's socks match and it's past time to go. The roof is leaking, but you don't have insurance. You can't seem to stop fighting with your spouse. Debt is piling up with no end in sight. You just found a hole in your favorite sweater.

There are lots of times when you won't feel able to conduct yourself in a manner worthy of the gospel. You may not feel able to conduct yourself in a manner worthy of anything useful at all. You'd rather just curl up in the dryer and permanent press yourself to death, or at least take a long nap.

Yet Paul's words were not directed to individuals going through life alone. Paul's words were to the body of believers. He urges them to be "striving together as one for the faith of the gospel" (v. 27).

In times of trouble and opposition, you don't have to go it alone. It can be scary to share your problems with others, it's true. But in order to live in a manner that reflects the gospel of Christ, at some point you've got to let go of your personal fears and lean into the body for protection, care, and support. You've got to love one another and be loved.

*Dear Lord, I'm having a rotten day. Help me to be
a good witness for Christ anyway. Amen. —ML*

PRAYING FOR THE GOSPEL

Join with me in suffering for the gospel, by the power of God.
2 TIMOTHY 1:8

One of the most important Christian duties is to tell others about Christ—to spread the gospel message. This is a primary goal, not because doing so will gain us points in heaven or a better pew position. It is a fulfillment of the two commands that Jesus said all of God's law hangs on—to love God (by working to expand His kingdom) and to love others (by telling them about the love of Christ).

You may not be called to spread the gospel in another language in a country far away. Yet you can help those who are. You can pray for them. You can ask God for their protection. You can ask God to give them courage and boldness. You can ask God to give them wisdom—to know when to speak and when not to, when to stand out and when to blend in.

Though you may not be called to deliver the gospel in foreign lands, you may be surprised to find yourself an ambassador for God in your own community. Just because a place is blessed with a church on every block does not necessarily mean all its residents understand the message of love and grace that the gospel carries with it.

Pray for an opportunity every day to share the gospel or to support those who do.

Dear Lord, help me to spread Your good news around the world. Amen. —ML

PRAYING FOR OUR NATION

For as the soil makes the sprout come up and a garden causes seeds to grow, so the Sovereign LORD will make righteousness and praise spring up before all nations.
ISAIAH 61:11

America is free, yes, but in other ways, we're far from it. We are, in fact, in bondage, oppressed by sin. We have chosen the easy road. Prejudice over justice. Convenience over life. We have chosen pleasure over goodness and duplicity over integrity. Our families are broken, and we're no longer even sure what a marriage or a family should look like. We are no longer concerned about what God has to say. People have heard of the Bible, but they don't read it for guidance. Because of these neglectful acts, our society is guilty of calling good evil, and evil good. We are indeed a fallen land, but we have chosen to fall even further.

This is a crucial time to pray for America, and there are many good scriptures to help you pray for our nation. Here is one to get you started, which is from Romans: "That the creation itself will be liberated from its bondage to decay and brought into the freedom and glory of the children of God" (8:21).

Lord God, protect this country from the disastrous effects of sin. Empower and equip Your children to rise up and show Christ's love to a lost and hurting world. Amen. —AH

CLOTHES STRAIGHT OUT OF THE DRYER

For this is what the LORD says: "I will extend peace to her like a river, and the wealth of nations like a flooding stream; you will nurse and be carried on her arm and dandled on her knees. As a mother comforts her child, so will I comfort you."
ISAIAH 66:12–13

It is 101 degrees outside. You're sweating even indoors. And yet when that dryer buzzer goes off and you scoop up those clothes out of the machine, you suddenly have an overwhelming urge to sit on the couch and bury yourself in a cocoon made from that load of clothes.

Hmm. Now why is that?

It feels like a comforting sanctuary, far from the madding crowd. It feels like what the world should be but isn't—warm, welcoming, and safe. Perhaps we should think of prayer in that way. The book of Isaiah tells us that as a mother comforts her child, so will God comfort us. That He will extend peace to us like a river.

So, the next time you're submerged inside the haven of a load of clothes straight from the dryer, think of God's love and wrap yourself in a cocoon of prayer. It's safe and welcoming, a most comforting place to be.

Father, thank You for caring about all of my needs—both great and small. You are my safe place, my constant refuge. Thank You for hearing me. Amen. —AH

THE ONLY
WAY TO TRAVEL

Cast all your anxiety on him
because he cares for you.
1 PETER 5:7

When humans experience emotional hurts and troubles, we tend to absorb them in an unhealthy way. Instead of giving them to God to deal with, we store them away in our hearts like travelers depositing items in their luggage. The problem is our spirits were never meant to deal with so much pain, and so we begin to feel downtrodden as we carry that ever-increasing load around. We get kind of crazy too, as we start to fling our baggage about, hurting other people with it.

Yes, humans are lousy travelers. Oh, we go here and there on planes and trains and automobiles, and we have fun and take photos and go home with nice memories, but we can't seem to get the spiritual journey right. That's because we're trying to do it alone.

The only way to travel this earth without dragging all of our various anxieties around is to cast them on Jesus—not just when the load gets so heavy that we've collapsed in a dead heap. But every day. Christ has already journeyed through this world, and He came out on the other side triumphant. He can help us to travel light.

Oh, and He has the perfect guidebook too!

God, give me the courage and faith to
give You control of every part of my life.
I can't do this without You. Amen. —AH

PRAYER VERSUS MEDITATION

Rather, he delights in the teachings of the
LORD and reflects on his teachings day and night.
PSALM 1:2 GW

On the topic of prayer versus meditation, there needs to be clarity. When the Bible speaks of reflection or meditation, it is not referring to meditation that encourages its participants to empty their minds. This type of meditation is at the heart of spiritual practices within non-Christian religions.

An empty mind is not a way to spiritual understanding but an invitation to what's unholy. During our quiet times, let us think on good and lovely things. Let us focus on God's Word, His truths, and His ways.

We shouldn't succumb to a desire to be trendy in our faith over a desire to please the one true God. While other religions and ancient traditions seem inviting—with their alluring promises of harmony and enlightenment—remember that biblical wisdom teaches us to beware of false prophets, to use discernment through the power of the Holy Spirit, and to weigh everything in light of God's holy Word.

Never does God encourage us to empty our minds. It is an increasingly popular spiritual practice, but don't be deceived—it is not biblical. Instead, these rituals are another attempt by the enemy of our souls to direct us away from the truth—from the power of real prayer.

Let us focus on what is biblical, what is holy, what is everlasting.

Lord, help me to pray and study Your Word in
a way that is pleasing to You. Amen. —AH

STANDING
OUT IN A CROWD

Be kind and compassionate to one another,
forgiving each other, just as in Christ God forgave you.
EPHESIANS 4:32

In a world of billions of people, we sometimes feel like one tiny grain of sand in a desert full of dunes. We long to rise up, to stand out—to achieve greatness. But we don't have to write a bestselling novel or win a gold medal in the Olympics or become president of the US to stand out in the crowd. It's as easy as one simple word. . . .

Kindness.

The impact of one kind deed can change a life forever, even if we only offer a sincere smile. Kindness has a ripple effect that can keep on flowing around the world. We might never know the full impact of our kind deeds. Yet God knows.

Paul's letter to the Ephesians tells us to be kind and compassionate to one another, forgiving each other, just as in Christ God forgave us.

But you might argue that kindness is not easy in a world that is becoming increasingly hardened and cruel. You're right—kindness isn't always easy. But it is good, just as God is good. We are to be compassionate and forgiving and kind because Christ has done the same for us.

Praying for a kind heart is a great way to start the day—it's beneficial for our own spirits and for every living soul who comes our way.

Jesus, mold me into a greater likeness
of You. Give me supernatural stores of
patience and compassion. Amen. —AH

A CASHMERE
KIND OF LIFE

*Because of the LORD's great love we are not
consumed, for his compassions never fail. They are
new every morning; great is your faithfulness.*
LAMENTATIONS 3:22–23

You save your money to buy that incredibly soft and amazingly feminine cashmere sweater—the one you've seen at the fancy dress shop in the mall. When you finally buy that dreamy sweater and slip it on, you do indeed think life might lead you to a place of perfection.

But then it happens—the unthinkable—a big ugly blob of ketchup propels itself onto that sweater like a missile. Then while you're busy trying to hide that stain with a scarf, you start to notice little nubs forming, and then there's that loose thread which threatens to undo the whole sweater. Soon that beautiful garment looks shabby, like it belongs at a rummage sale instead of a fine dress shop.

We are forever searching for a cashmere life in a mire-soaked world. Not just in the material world, but in our spiritual lives. This human drama—this soul quest—ceased two thousand years ago. The answer is here, and His name is Jesus Christ. He came not only to help us in our hour of need but to give us life eternal.

He is faithful and His mercies are new every morning, so let us pray for a fresh start and a clean heart.

*Dear Lord Jesus, You alone are the source of true
refreshment and new beginnings. Help me to
run to You when I feel ragged. Amen.* —AH

A SUPERNATURAL REALM

For our struggle is not against flesh and blood,
but against the rulers, against the authorities,
against the powers of this dark world and against
the spiritual forces of evil in the heavenly realms.
EPHESIANS 6:12

Since we have a keen familiarity with our material world, it's hard to imagine a supernatural realm that exists beyond the borders of our sensory experiences. But the Bible says that there is much more to this life than flesh and blood. More than what we merely see with our eyes.

There is a spiritual domain as well, and it's as real as the rocks and the trees and the clouds—and us. Yes, this can be a dark world; and we struggle against the spiritual forces of evil, which include Satan and his emissaries. If you are truly honest with yourself, you know in your spirit that this is truth.

So, how can we deal with such evil? In Ephesians, it reads, "Stand firm then, with the belt of truth buckled around your waist, with the breastplate of righteousness in place, and with your feet fitted with the readiness that comes from the gospel of peace" (6:14–15).

We can stand firm and love God.

We can live by His Word and His truths.

And we can pray like there is no tomorrow.

Holy Spirit, help me to always be aware of
the spiritual forces in this world. Give me the
strength and power to face them. Amen. —AH

YOU ARE
NEVER ALONE

He took Peter and the two sons of Zebedee along with him, and he began to be sorrowful and troubled. Then he said to them, "My soul is overwhelmed with sorrow to the point of death. Stay here and keep watch with me."
MATTHEW 26:37–38

The night is a hundred shades of black, and it has nothing to do with nightfall. Your spirit is crushed, and you feel utterly abandoned. Sometimes life is that dark—it can feel that hopeless.

It is a great comfort to know that you are not alone in the midst of life's horror. Jesus grew up here on earth and He must have known many of the usual trials and triumphs of a childhood. Yet when He became a man and faced His divine destiny, Christ knew the black flood of suffering—pain and anguish we cannot even imagine. He said, "My soul is overwhelmed with sorrow to the point of death." Jesus' agony was so very great, He sweat drops of blood.

When despair comes to us, be comforted in the knowledge that Jesus knows torment as deep and lonely as the darkest reaches of hell. In your hour of need, He will hold you in the palm of His hand, because He understands like no one else. Because He loves you. He always has loved you—enough to die for you.

When you pray, know this truth—you are never ever alone in that dark night.

Father, in times of great despair, shield and sustain me. Be my hiding place and my source of supernatural comfort and peace. Amen. —AH

THOSE WHO
BRING GOOD NEWS

*How, then, can they call on the one they have
not believed in? And how can they believe in
the one of whom they have not heard? And
how can they hear without someone preaching
to them? And how can anyone preach unless
they are sent? As it is written: "How beautiful
are the feet of those who bring good news!"*
Romans 10:14–15

In our modern world, there has been much concern about the carbon footprint we leave behind as humans. When God created our earth, He did indeed ask us to be good stewards of His beautiful world, but over the years our priorities have shifted; we now focus more intensely on the needs of our planet rather than the needs of people and their souls.

As Christians, when we leave this earth and come to meet our maker face-to-face, He won't be as concerned about whether we recycled as much as whether we obeyed His mandate of sharing the gospel. Did we spend our days worrying about our carbon footprint or more of our time dealing with the eternal imprint that we were able to leave by sharing the good news of Christ?

Let us always pray for opportunities to share the mercy and love of our Savior with people of all nations—whether it's our neighbors overseas or simply our neighbors across the street.

*Lord, remind me of my calling as a Christian.
Equip me with the words to say and give me the
boldness to carry out Your plan. Amen.* —AH

IF YOU LOVE
ONE ANOTHER

*"By this everyone will know that you are
my disciples, if you love one another."*
JOHN 13:35

That checker at the grocery store who doesn't seem very friendly may not be a snob; she may just be hard of hearing. That gal who cut you off in traffic may not have been trying to ruin your day; she might have been too blurry-eyed from tears to see your car. And even if folks really do choose to be stuck-up and rude, as Christians, our reaction should be different than that of the world. We would never want to grieve the Holy Spirit by flinging out sharp barbs and hateful deeds. Both *hate* and *love* are simple four-letter words, and yet they couldn't be more different in spirit.

Hate speaks volumes.

Love speaks volumes.

Hate is so easy that anyone can do it. It takes no effort. No education. No courage. And if you make an ongoing habit of it, your soul may be so deadened that you have little conscience left. Eventually, you'll look into the face of hate and say, "Yeah. We're good." At first, hate may be an easy and wide road to travel, but it is a path that can only lead to destruction.

Hate's counterpart—love—takes patience and practice and much prayer. Yet it will bring a lightness of spirit to you and to everyone around you. It will bring joy and peace and a good night's sleep.

What is your heart prayer?

*God, teach me how to turn away from hate
and to always choose love. Amen.* —AH

THE HEART THAT CHOOSES JOY

Rejoice in the Lord always. I will say it again: Rejoice!
PHILIPPIANS 4:4

Sometimes life feels like a garish circus ride through a shadowy pit of doom—and that's on a good day! When we plop on the couch in front of the TV screen, the *last* thing we feel like doing is rejoicing.

Hmm. Your head aches from a traffic jam. You spilled coffee on your new dress. Your hair isn't cooperating. It never does. Your friend canceled lunch—again. On top of that you dread telling your husband that you dropped your cell phone in the mud. When you finally get home, you just want to be left alone on the couch to vegetate. Right?

Yet God says to rejoice. We are not expected to celebrate the unhappy circumstances in life, but we can have joy in the midst of them. Try picking ten things in your life that you're grateful for, and then during your prayer time, rejoice in your heart by thanking God for these blessings. Thank Him for His goodness. His gift of eternal life. His faithfulness. His mercies are new every morning.

A soul filled with the world's mindset will wilt, but a heart that chooses holy joy will look up, and it will be renewed.

*Father, help me to think on Your goodness
and provision instead of my worries and
frustrations. Thank You for Your love,
mercy, and patience. Amen. —AH*

OH, WHEN SPRING COMES

*Therefore, if anyone is in Christ, the new
creation has come: The old has gone, the new is here!*
2 CORINTHIANS 5:17

Oh, when spring comes—the earth celebrates with newness. We see green sprouting up everywhere in every shade imaginable. Those budding leaves almost seem to have an illumination of their own. The melting snow floods the brooks, and the water tumbles down the mountains, spraying rainbows across the canyons. Spring, ahh, the flowers are peeking out their little heads, the bunnies are hopping about, the sun is warm, the breeze is silk, and the birds are nesting and singing their little hearts out. What could be more refreshing, inviting, and wonderful?

When spring comes we think of the words *flourish, growth, expectations, possibilities, hope, newness,* and *promise.* That is the way with Christ. He brings those qualities to us when we become His, when we walk with Him, when we come to know Him through fellowship and His Word. We become new like spring. The old is gone, and the new is here.

Talk to God today, and let the newness of spring into your heart, into your life.

*Lord, thank You for loving me and for washing away
my sins. Help me to live as a new creation, that I
might trust in Your will, have hope in Your Word, and
treat others as I would like to be treated. Amen. —AH*

WHAT IS PARAMOUNT?

"Again, truly I tell you that if two of you on earth agree about anything they ask for, it will be done for them by my Father in heaven. For where two or three gather in my name, there am I with them."
MATTHEW 18:19–20

Calling out to God anywhere and anytime is appropriate, and yet one scenario we should never forget is to pray along with other believers. When two or more gather in the name of Christ, the Bible says God will give us what we need. If we come into alignment with His will, then our requests will take on a righteous and heavenly scope. Within His plan and surrounded by godly people, our petitions will become focused on what is truly needed rather than every whim of our hearts.

Only God can know what we truly need. What if we were to beg Him for a big house in a gated community, but that lifestyle would cause us—little by little—to become so fashionable and self-centered and exclusive behind those gated walls that we could no longer do His will or even wish to do His will? Only He can know all the wiles of Satan. Only He can know all the ways we might be tempted to fall into sin. Therefore, seeking God's will for our lives is not just a helpful suggestion.

It is paramount.

God, even when life doesn't go my way, help me to trust in Your plan and to remember that You know the desires of my heart. Amen. —AH

GENTLE AND
HUMBLE OF HEART

*But God chose the foolish things of the world to
shame the wise; God chose the weak things of the
world to shame the strong. God chose the lowly
things of this world and the despised things—and the
things that are not—to nullify the things that are.*
1 CORINTHIANS 1:27–28

Throughout the Bible, we see God selecting people for His tasks who might be considered by the world's standards to be very unwise choices. Yet God does not see people the way we see them. He may pick someone—whom the world despises because of a lack of wealth or fame or academic accolades or clever wit or worldly savvy—and raise her up to show a haughty society just how foolish their pride looks.

The Gospel of Matthew says, "Blessed are the meek, for they will inherit the earth" (5:5). Jesus called Himself gentle and humble of heart. So, if you are feeling unfit for duty because you are humble and lowly by the world's standards, take heart. God loves the meek. If you feel you are lacking in a gentle and selfless spirit, just ask God for one, and He would be pleased to give it to you.

*Father, thank You for loving misfits,
outcasts, and sinners. Cultivate in me
a spirit of humility. Amen. —AH*

GOD NEVER FAILS

Then Moses said to them, "No one is to keep any of it until morning." However, some of them paid no attention to Moses; they kept part of it until morning, but it was full of maggots and began to smell. So Moses was angry with them.
EXODUS 16:19–20

In Exodus we find that the Israelites went against God's command and gathered more manna than what they needed for each day. It was obvious that the Israelites didn't trust the Almighty. Even though they had witnessed wondrous miracles, they assumed God would forget about them. So, they took precautions.

How is that different from the way we treat God today? We desire the security of a bigger bank account and more space in our homes than we can use. We want more clothes than we can wear. More food than we can eat. We want assurances for the future. If God wants to come alongside our plans and our stockpiling, well, all the better.

God wants us to prayerfully trust Him to supply our needs. We must work, yes, but we shouldn't get ahead of God. Just like with the Israelites, He wants us to know that walking alongside Him is the safest place to be. The wisest place. The securities and promises of this world ring hollow. Banks close and kingdoms fall.

God never fails.

Lord, help me to find my security in You and not in the fickle, fleeting things of this world. Amen. —AH

COME INTO
HIS PRESENCE

*Even though I walk through the darkest valley,
I will fear no evil, for you are with me; your rod
and your staff, they comfort me. You prepare a
table before me in the presence of my enemies.
You anoint my head with oil; my cup overflows.*
PSALM 23:4–5

When you wake up in the morning, do you feel like your spiritual tank is empty or, at best, you're running on fumes? The world has plenty of soul-fuel of every kind, but it's like putting water into a gas tank. You can open the garage door to drive away, but the car won't take you where you need to go.

God says if we come into His presence, He will give us rest. He will give us peace that passes all understanding—something the world cannot give, cannot even comprehend. He will lead us beside quiet waters, giving us comfort in times of trial. We will fear no evil when He is near. He will refresh our souls and guide us along the right paths. When we make Him our daily Shepherd, we will lack for nothing.

In fact, when we're in His presence, we'll find that our spirit's cup will overflow—with joy and love and strength for the day.

Prayer.

It's the best soul-fuel money can't buy.

*Father, help me to make fellowship with
You my top priority. You are the only true
source of peace, joy, and fulfillment in a
world full of counterfeits. Amen. —AH*

EXPECTATION

"Ask and it will be given to you; seek and you will find; knock and the door will be opened to you. For everyone who asks receives; the one who seeks finds; and to the one who knocks, the door will be opened."
MATTHEW 7:7–8

The candles are aglow on the birthday cake, soft and flickering and golden. The packages are stacked just so, all wrapped in festive papers and bows. Your child's eyes are lit with anticipation of good things, delight, and wonder.

When we call on the Lord for help and mercy, we can come into His presence with expectation. In His Word He promises to hear our prayers, to open the door to us, to give us what we need. The Gospel of Matthew goes on to say, "Which of you, if your son asks for bread, will give him a stone? Or if he asks for a fish, will give him a snake? If you, then, though you are evil, know how to give good gifts to your children, how much more will your Father in heaven give good gifts to those who ask him!" (vv. 9–11).

Of course, the gifts that the Lord chooses to give us might be wisdom or forgiveness or peace or joy. These gifts may not be material, but they are timeless. So, like a child on her birthday, come to Christ with anticipation of good things, delight, and wonder!

Father, thank You for all of the wonderful gifts You've given me. I have hope in Your loving provision. Amen. —AH

THE GIFT

One of them, when he saw he was healed, came back, praising God in a loud voice. He threw himself at Jesus' feet and thanked him—and he was a Samaritan. Jesus asked, "Were not all ten cleansed? Where are the other nine? Has no one returned to give praise to God except this foreigner?" Then he said to him, "Rise and go; your faith has made you well."
LUKE 17:15–19

Ever need a vacation after a vacation? When we finally get away on a trip, it's easy to gorge ourselves on sights and experiences. We cram so much into the hours and even minutes of our trip that we forget to stop and breathe. To truly appreciate the gift of the moment.

It's easy to live life the same way. Never slowing down to breathe. Grabbing all we can get while the getting is good. Not taking the time to look up with a heart of thanksgiving.

Perhaps that is what happened to the other nine men in the Bible who forgot to come back and thank Jesus for His gift of healing. It appears that they were so busy getting on with their lives that they forgot to thank the one who'd set them free. The one who'd given them their lives back. It only takes a moment out of our busy day to thank the giver of all good gifts.

What blessing can we thank the Lord for today?

God, thank You for setting me free and giving me the gift of eternal life. You have blessed me more than I can fathom. Amen. —AH

A TREE PLANTED
BY THE WATER

*"But blessed is the one who trusts in the LORD,
whose confidence is in him. They will be like a
tree planted by the water that sends out its roots
by the stream. It does not fear when heat comes;
its leaves are always green. It has no worries in a
year of drought and never fails to bear fruit."*
JEREMIAH 17:7–8

The streams have dried up. The land is barren. Rain is only a memory.
The cicadas may be the only thing left singing. Have you ever experienced this kind of serious drought? If you have, it is unforgettable.
Drought is a brutal force of nature—an unforgiving taskmaster. That
is the way of the world. It will steal your strength until you are weak
and vulnerable and fruitless.

Yet prayer can build up our trust in the Lord. He is our strength
in a harsh and desolate land. If we faithfully spend time with Him
and His good Word, we will be like that tree in the book of Jeremiah.
We will be that tree planted by the water that sends out its roots by
the stream. A tree that does not fear the heat or a year of drought.
It's the kind of tree that will never fail to bear fruit.

So, what kind of tree are you?

*Lord, when I'm feeling lost and dried up, give me the
strength to turn to You with outstretched arms and to
have faith in Your goodness and love. Amen. —AH*

HOPE
ARRIVED ONE NIGHT

The Word became flesh and made his dwelling
among us. We have seen his glory. . .who came
from the Father, full of grace and truth.

JOHN 1:14

Imagine no chapel bells ringing clear on a crisp winter day. Imagine no Christmas trees glittering with lights, no carols of celebration, no angelic host to proclaim hope to mankind.

Now, imagine—no empty tomb.

No forgiveness. No mercy. No hope of heaven or freedom from darkness. It would be a world forever trapped in spiritual nightfall with no promise of dawn. But God didn't choose to leave us in our sin. Because of our Creator's love for us, hope arrived one night in a small bundle in a lowly place—a baby whose name was Immanuel, which in Hebrew means "God is with us." Yes, it was a simple birth, but it was also grace filled. It was a sacred night that would change the course of human history.

JESUS. He is the only hope this broken world has ever known. The book of Isaiah tells us, "And he will be called Wonderful Counselor, Mighty God, Everlasting Father, Prince of Peace" (9:6).

What a mighty Savior. What hope everlasting!

The nativity scene and the empty tomb should become more to us than mere historical highlights and entertaining holidays. Let them become truths that transform our minds and hearts—not just once a year during Christmas, but every day. In every prayer.

Jesus, thank You for making Yourself poor
by coming down to earth so that I could be
made rich by Your grace. Amen. —AH

A WORLD IN PERIL

*For our struggle is not against flesh and blood,
but against the rulers, against the authorities,
against the powers of this dark world and against
the spiritual forces of evil in the heavenly realms.*
EPHESIANS 6:12

If you've ever faced evil—and we all have—you know how it looks. It is ugly and terrifying. However, it might also be just a little bit enticing. It makes one shudder, but at the same time, it might make us take a peek around the corner for just one more look.

We are in a spiritual tug-of-war; and like in a real battle, the enemy and his dark battalion are intent on destroying us, especially the part of us that matters the most—our very souls.

Our world is in peril. What can we do? Perhaps it is time for us to be like the title of that beloved hymn. "Rise Up, O Saints of God!"

The book of Ephesians gives us a warning—almost like a battle cry—when it says, "Therefore put on the full armor of God, so that when the day of evil comes, you may be able to stand your ground, and after you have done everything, to stand. Stand firm then, with the belt of truth buckled around your waist, with the breastplate of righteousness in place" (vv. 13–14).

In this deadly spiritual battle for our souls, which side do you stand on?

What prayer is on your heart in these perilous times?

*God, help me to stand firm in Your truth and
light. Shield me from Satan's lies. Amen.* —AH

THESE
SACRED WORDS

One day Jesus was praying in a certain place. When he finished, one of his disciples said to him, "Lord, teach us to pray, just as John taught his disciples."

LUKE 11:1

Imagine being taught how to pray by God Himself? What an inspiring event in history. Did the disciples comprehend the majesty of the moment? Did they know these sacred words would transcend time, that they would virtually crackle the air like lightning every time they were spoken, that they would contain enough supernatural power to alter every human heart? Surely they must have known the awesome significance of that holy lesson on prayer.

Here is Jesus' prayer as it appears in the Gospel of Matthew: "Our Father in heaven, hallowed be your name, your kingdom come, your will be done, on earth as it is in heaven. Give us today our daily bread. And forgive us our debts, as we also have forgiven our debtors. And lead us not into temptation, but deliver us from the evil one" (6:9–13).

There are many right ways to pray, but isn't it a joyous thing, an awesome privilege, to be taught how to pray by the one who made us? The one who longs to be with us? Who wants to someday take that conversation you're having with Him right into eternity?

Lord, thank You for teaching me how to pray. Please give me more discipline in my prayer life. Make my communion with You more essential to me than food. Amen. —AH

THE SEASON
OF SINGING

"See! The winter is past; the rains are over and gone.
Flowers appear on the earth; the season of singing
has come, the cooing of doves is heard in our land."
SONG OF SONGS 2:11–12

Is your life caught up in a cold winter that never seems to end? Then snuggle up in a warm blanket of truth.

God may allow you to stay in that winter season for now, but He will never leave your side. He will stay with you and bring you all that you need. He'll send the comforting presence of the Holy Spirit. He provides you with His mighty Word to heat and stir your soul. He offers you the safe and sheltering knowledge of eternal life through Christ. Under the lamp of these truths we can sing in our hearts, knowing spring is near.

In time, the cold will go. The ice will thaw. The rain will cease, and the sun will burst boldly through the clouds in rays of pure gold. The earth will turn a lush green, and flowers will spring up in a profusion of color. Even the gentle cooing of doves will be heard all through the land. What beauty. What hope. What joy.

In times of winter, let us pray and seek His face, and know too that the season of singing will indeed come again.

God, give me joy and patience in the long winters of
life. Remind me of Your steadfast presence, and may
Your Word strengthen and comfort me. Amen. —AH

PLAYING
IN THE MUD

*However, as it is written: "What no eye has
seen, what no ear has heard, and what no
human mind has conceived"—the things God
has prepared for those who love him.*
1 CORINTHIANS 2:9

Did you ever make mud pies and cakes when you were little? Pretty
fun stuff, eh? Interesting to think that all the time we were mixing and
shaping and generally mucking around, we were envisioning something much grander. We had the hope that when we were finished
baking our mud in the sun that it might be somehow transformed
into a spectacular three-tiered wedding cake. When in reality it was
only mud decorated with leaves and twigs.

As adults, we know that all we create can be beautiful, exquisite
really, but it is still only a shadow of what's to come for those who
live in Christ. We are still only children playing in the mud. But with
the hope of glorious things to come.

When we pray, let it be with the eyes of heaven, knowing and
believing full well what is to come. Someday the earthly vision, this
promise of more, will no longer be a shadow or a dream.

It will be real.

*Dear Jesus, as I live out my life on earth, help me
to never forget my true, eternal home in heaven.
I was made for more than mud. You created
me for beauty, freedom, joy, and an intimate,
unbroken fellowship with You. Amen. —AH*

HORNET OR
BUTTERFLY?

*Therefore, if anyone is in Christ, the new creation
has come: The old has gone, the new is here!*
2 CORINTHIANS 5:17

You've seen this woman coming, and invariably there is fear and
trembling in her wake. When she arrives in the break room at work,
people suddenly part like the Red Sea. This woman wakes up ready
for a fight. She relishes the idea of annihilating someone with her
"looks" and slashing someone with her sharp tongue. That angry
woman might even be the woman who sits down next to you in
church. On occasions—rare, of course—that woman might be you
or me! *Oh dear!*

What to do?

We can ask ourselves each and every morning who we will be
that day—an ornery hornet with a sting that brings tears and pain,
or a butterfly that flutters on people's hands, making them smile with
delight. Sound impossible? It would be hard to change using our
own willpower, but this new attitude can be accomplished through
the power of the Holy Spirit. In 2 Corinthians, it tells us that when
we accept Christ, we are a new creation. Let us pray that the Holy
Spirit will make us new every morning. That when we go out into
the world, we will have the supernatural power to be all that is good
and lovely. And that there will be no angry hornets among us!

*God, within You alone lies the power for true
transformation and growth. Help me to reflect
Your glory to a world in need. Amen.* —AH

EVEN MORE BEAUTIFUL

The righteous cry out, and the LORD hears them;
he delivers them from all their troubles. The LORD is
close to the brokenhearted and saves those who are
crushed in spirit. The righteous person may have many
troubles, but the LORD delivers him from them all.
PSALM 34:17–19

There is an amazing Japanese art form in which an artist will take broken pottery and painstakingly glue it back together with a lacquer resin. This resin is mixed or dusted with powdered metals, such as silver or gold. This creative technique will take what was once broken and unusable and transform it into something even more beautiful than it was before.

God Almighty, the master craftsman, can and does that very thing for each of us if we ask Him. When we cry out to God, when we trust Him, He will take our shattered lives and remake them into works of genius. God is a master of redemption as well as creation, and because of His love for us, He wants to not only make us new but make us even more exquisite than we ever imagined. He wants to give us daily purpose and soul beauty as well as eternal hope.

That kind of redemption, that kind of miraculous re-creation is ours, and it's only a prayer away.

Father, thank You for the boundless power of Your
redemption. Recreate, restore, refresh, and redeem
me from the clutches of death and sin. Amen. —AH

WHO HOLDS
THE TRUTH?

*And no wonder, for Satan himself
masquerades as an angel of light.*
2 CORINTHIANS 11:14

Everybody is selling some kind of spiritual truth. Even if a person doesn't believe in God, that belief system is still a creed to live by—a conviction that requires faith.

There are many kinds of religions and cults to choose from in the marketplace of ideas, and all of them claim to carry the light. But remember, this is a supernatural world, and Satan, the enemy of your soul, would love nothing better than to whisper all manner of lies into your spirit and so blind and dazzle you that it becomes easier not to recognize the truth and light when it does come.

How can we be safe in a world full of people who shout their spiritual wares at every corner like callers at a carnival arcade? Who masquerade as light bearers? We can attend a Bible-believing church. We can read God's Word so that we can recognize false prophets. We can pray for discernment, that we might know when someone comes to us with "tweaks" on the never-changing gospel of Christ. That is, alterations in God's truth that might appease sinful man but not honor a righteous God.

God has given us free will. What is our prayerful choice?

*Lord, help me to stand strong in Your truth and to not
be enticed by the popular, fickle views of man. I want
to stay within the light of Your Word. Amen. —AH*

GRABBER HOGS

For although they knew God, they neither glorified him as God nor gave thanks to him, but their thinking became futile and their foolish hearts were darkened.

ROMANS 1:21

So, what is a grabber hog anyway? Some people would say it's a lifestyle—an insatiable appetite for more of everything. The problem is the more we get, the more we want. Sometimes we treat God like we're ordering up room service at a hotel. While we're still eating, we're already planning the next feast. While we pay off one credit card, we're already window-shopping for more dainty desires. And waiting? Forget it. We want what we want when we want it. After all, the world says we can have it all. Right?

The Bible clearly tells us that we can make our requests known to God. He cares very much for our needs. And yet, there is more to prayer than the material world and what we want right now. There is thanksgiving, praise, repentance, praying for the needs of others; there is listening to that still, small voice for knowledge and guidance, for peace, and for strength for the day. And there is tender communion.

Ask Him for a change in our hearts' desires—that they will be aligned with His—and the need to have it all will be replaced with something more lasting, more treasured. Doesn't the word *contentment* have a sweeter feel to it than the world's "grabber hog" philosophy?

Father, forgive me for neglecting to thank You for all that You've given me. Give me a spirit of contentment, that I might praise and thank You in all circumstances. Amen. —AH

FINDING HOME

Then Jesus told them this parable: "Suppose one of you
has a hundred sheep and loses one of them. Doesn't
he leave the ninety-nine in the open country and go
after the lost sheep until he finds it? And when he finds
it, he joyfully puts it on his shoulders and goes home."
LUKE 15:3–6

A child, who was right by her mother's side, disappears at the airport terminal. The little girl is suddenly amid a sea of strangers, turning around and searching, frightened and lost. This scenario is one of the most terrifying moments in a mother's life, because she cannot bear to be separated from her beloved child when she knows the child is stranded and confused and in danger. The mother will do anything to bring her back.

So it is with Christ, who did do everything for us to bring us back from our wandering. Not only is He reaching out to you, but He gave up His life so that He could take you home.

We are so much like the lost sheep that the Bible talks about. Yet Jesus, the Good Shepherd, desires that none should perish, so He will go to the ends of the earth to find you and bring you back.

What will be your response? Will you run into His arms? Will there be tears of joy? What will you say?

Jesus, thank You for pursuing me as a shepherd
pursues his lost sheep. Guide me back to the
safety of Your loving embrace. Amen. —AH

NEW EVERY MORNING

Because of the LORD's great love we are not consumed,
for his compassions never fail. They are new every
morning; great is your faithfulness. I say to myself,
"The LORD is my portion; therefore I will wait for him."
LAMENTATIONS 3:22–24

People love all things new and fresh.

A crisp new linen tablecloth whipped up in the air and smoothed down just right for the arrival of one's guests. A snowfall that covers a dingy landscape, transforming it into pristine and dazzling loveliness. The rosy blush of a newborn infant cooing her way into your heart. The sun rising in a new dawn, bringing with it a symphony of color and light. A bride walking down the aisle, dressed in white and drenched in love. Such beauty and promise is in all things new.

The old is past. The new has come. Oh, how that inspires us. It should move us. The Lord promises that His compassions never fail. They are new every morning. He assures us that His faithfulness is beyond the ordinary—it's extraordinary!

What can we do in this new dawn that will help celebrate this fresh start? An apology to someone we've wronged? Connecting with someone who feels lost? Extending forgiveness to others and to ourselves? A helping hand? Or perhaps quiet time spent with the Savior who wants to make your heart new and your soul refreshed again?

Lord, help me to wake up every day with a content,
refreshed spirit, equipped to encounter any
storms because You are with me. Amen. —AH

THE MOUSE
IN THE MAZE

Give thanks to the LORD, for he is
good; his love endures forever.
1 CHRONICLES 16:34

Have you ever felt like a mouse trapped in a maze? You go around in circles, and you can't find your way out? Perhaps you have a financial situation that keeps coming back like an unwelcome guest. Maybe you're estranged from your family with no hope of reconciliation. Perhaps the doctor gave you test results that were an ugly surprise. Maybe your boss says that if you don't work harder and faster you'll lose your job.

Do the days seem endless, and do the nights seem riddled with bad dreams—that is, if you ever get to sleep at all?

What a place to be. There is no one exempt from trials in this fallen world—these life moments that make you feel stuck and more than a little sick at heart. If you do find yourself trapped, and there is no place else to go but to your knees, and there's nowhere else to be but at the mercy of God, well, it's a mighty good place to find yourself. The Lord will never fail.

Seek Him now, whether you're on the mountaintop or you feel trapped in the deepest, darkest maze.

God is good. His love and His mercy endure forever.

Count on it.

Father God, I surrender to Your care and Your will.
You are my mighty Redeemer, my stronghold and
comforter. Oh, how I need You. Amen. —AH

MS. KNOW-IT-ALL

*All Scripture is God-breathed and is
useful for teaching, rebuking, correcting
and training in righteousness.*
2 TIMOTHY 3:16

Ms. Know-it-all. Oww-wee, she can really put a serious snag in your pantyhose.

You've seen her in action. She's the expert in everything, even if she isn't. She thinks correction is something for her eyesight, not her soul. This character trait can spell misery everywhere she goes.

So, what is this woman's problem? She is not a teachable person—and what's worse—she may not even know it. That is not how God wants us to interact with our fellow man, and certainly not how we are to approach the Almighty. No matter how many theological degrees we have, no matter how impressive our IQ, no matter how humble we *think* we are, there are still discoveries to be made and much to learn. So, what happens when you find out that unteachable monster is you?

Study God's Word, because all scripture is God-breathed and is useful for teaching, rebuking, correcting, and training in righteousness. Pray that the Holy Spirit will transform your spiritual landscape into something growing and beautiful, something teachable and usable for His kingdom. This meek way of living is blessed; and not only will it bring joy to all those who touch your life, but joy will fill your own heart as well.

*Lord, soften my heart and make me
teachable. Transform me with the wisdom
of Your Word. Amen.* —AH

A FRIEND
LIKE NONE OTHER

"Before they call I will answer;
while they are still speaking I will hear."
ISAIAH 65:24

Just as honey makes the medicine taste better, so do good friends make this sometimes-bitter life go down more easily. If you've known what it's like to be friendless, it can be as lonely as a howling wind blowing across a desert. No one to understand you, to listen and *hear* you, to share your life with—especially in those special moments that cry out to be experienced with someone else and not just by yourself.

If you find yourself friendless, know that Jesus is a friend—the very best kind. He will not abandon you when times get tough. He is a wise, listening friend who will not merely tell you what you want to hear but what you need to hear. A friend who will help you carry your burdens, rejoice with you, laugh with you, weep with you, and love you always. He is a friend who says, "Before you call I will answer; while you are still speaking I will hear." Now isn't that the kind of wonderful fellowship our lonely hearts have searched for?

The old hymn "What a Friend We Have in Jesus" says it so beautifully.

What a friend we have in Jesus, All our sins and griefs to bear!
What a privilege to carry Everything to God in prayer!

Jesus, thank You for hearing me and for
calling me Your friend. Amen. —AH

A HARRIED LIFE

*Wait for the LORD; be strong and take
heart and wait for the LORD.*
PSALM 27:14

We learn at an early age to cut in line, to push ahead, even if it means knocking someone else out of the way. We live words like *scramble, rush, speed, frustration, nonstop, shove, frenzy, late, propel, time crunch, crisis, struggle,* and *commotion* just to name a few. Your pulse may have gone up just reading those words!

Why do we act in such a ridiculously harried, hurried way? We do it because we want to get to the next thing in life—as quickly as possible. But as soon as we arrive, we sprint to the next item on our agenda.

No time to slow down or take a breather, and the last thing on one's mind is waiting on the Lord. Well, there is an answer. It's called Sunday, which was a special day made for man. Sunday is a good time to spend some serious quality time with God, just sitting by a golden pond and talking to Him. Our souls will soon embrace words like *rest, calm, joy, divine, tranquility, reflection, breathing, wander, repose, communion, balance, sublime, inspired,* and *refreshed.*

Great words? Ahh, yes. Sunday is a great day to gather them in one's spirit like wildflowers in one's basket. Yes, a great day to wait on the Lord.

*God, help me to learn how to slow down and
be still. When I lose Your voice in the frantic
noise, be not far from me. Amen. —AH*

GETTING
DIRECTIONS

Your word is a lamp for my feet, a light on my path.
PSALM 119:105

Have you ever been lost? I mean *really* lost? So, you stop to ask for directions? It usually goes something like this. "Well, hon, it's easy-peasy. You just have to go down this zig-zaggy street right over there and then make a quick left at the third light, and then a quick right after the mini-mart. If you come to the bridge, you've gone too far. Oh, and there's a detour that will take you a few miles out of your way, but it shouldn't take too long." *Oh boy. I think I lost you at zig-zaggy.*

Yes, it's this kind of navigation nightmare that made GPS extremely popular.

Too bad there isn't a guide for living that works like GPS. Actually, there is. It's called the Word of God. When read faithfully, His good Word is like a lamp to our feet, or like a GPS in our car.

Before you begin your daily reading, ask the Holy Spirit to give you understanding. The Bible will indeed light your path, and if you love Him and follow Him, He will not only help you navigate the rough and convoluted roads of this life; He'll ultimately lead you right where you need to be—heaven.

*Father, thank You for making Yourself
and Your will known to us through Your holy
Word. Help me to be diligent in my reading,
and open my eyes to Your truth. Amen. —AH*

ALL THE
PRETTY PEBBLES

*"Whoever tries to keep their life will lose it,
and whoever loses their life will preserve it."*
LUKE 17:33

Have you ever strolled along a stream, picking up pretty pebbles? The stones can be like finding treasures, and some of them sparkle like precious gems. Maybe you tend to gather so many that they start to spill from your hands, or you grasp them so tightly they make your fingers ache, or they weigh so heavily in your pockets that they become a burden instead of a blessing.

Isn't that just like our lives when we gather more than we can use and we cling too tightly to all that doesn't truly belong to us? Like our careers, our houses, our possessions, our families, our very lives. All belongs to God and all is under His authority, but that concept is hard for us to grasp, let alone embrace. In fact, it's at the heart of why mankind fell from grace. Humans want to own, control, and choose their own way.

God says we should not grasp too tightly to life or anything in it. It seems like such a paradox—that to lose is to gain. Yet it is the only way to live.

When we finally empty our pockets of all those pretty pebbles and release them to God's care, we will find a lighter way to travel life's road.

Pray for that kind of walk with the Lord, that kind of freedom.

*Holy Spirit, enable me to give You control,
and help me to live in freedom. Amen. —AH*

NOTHING I DESIRE

*Whom have I in heaven but you? And earth
has nothing I desire besides you.*
PSALM 73:25

There is no one like our God.

There is no king of heaven who waits for you, except Him. There is no creator God who cares for you, except Him. He alone made you and shaped you and caused you to grow. There is nothing on earth to desire that is like Him.

There is no one who can take your requests, answer your questions, or wipe away your sadness like God.

So when you look for fulfillment and completeness, for answers and forgiveness, you must make sure you are looking to God first and not get confused by other options. You must not mistake sources of good gifts on earth for the one great source who made every good gift. You must be careful to reach out, not to just any spiritual power, but to the Lord's all-powerful hands.

There are many voices out there in the world—begging for your attention. There are many ways to get deceived. To be clear-minded and alert and to filter out all the different messages, it's likely you'll need some help.

God is the strength of your heart. God is the strength of your mind and soul and body too. Ask Him to guide you, and He will. Bring your desires to Him, and He will make you complete.

*Dear God, there is no one like You!
I love You! Amen. —ML*

WATCH AND PRAY

"Watch and pray so that you will not fall into temptation. The spirit is willing, but the flesh is weak."
MARK 14:38

Jesus told His disciples to watch and pray. It was a tense time. He knew what was coming and the kind of fallout that would be heading toward His followers after His death on the cross. He wanted them to be on guard. He wanted them to pray with Him.

Watch and pray. Those two little verbs can be so hard to accomplish sometimes, can't they?

Sometimes it's the watching that is the very thing that gets us into trouble. We watch what's going on around us instead of watching out for temptation. We're like children in a toy store, getting distracted with all the colorful delights that would be so easy to grab.

Sometimes it's the praying that is the problem. The problem being, we just don't do it. We think about doing it. We put a time in our calendars to do it. We buy books about it and hear sermons about it. Every now and then in a group we might bow our heads and pretend to be listening. Yet none of that is actually doing the thing.

Watch and pray. The disciples found it hard to do, even for an hour. Put yourself in their shoes. Do you think you would have done any better?

Dear God, help me to be disciplined so I
can set my mind on You. Amen. —ML

IF

"If my people, who are called by my name, will humble themselves and pray. . .then I will hear from heaven."
2 CHRONICLES 7:14

Did your mom ever give you one of those never-ending "if" clauses as an answer to a request to go somewhere or do something? "Well, if you get your room cleaned up and if your homework is done and if dinner is ready on time and if. . ." You might think she never wanted to take you to the park/mall/toy store/wherever at all!

God gave a list of "if" clauses in His message to Solomon. But He was actually hoping His people *could* get these "ifs" accomplished. He wanted His people to humble themselves—perhaps a good reminder right after the people had just finished proudly celebrating the establishment of the temple of the Lord.

He wanted His people to seek His face and turn from their wicked ways. It's difficult to look for God if you are met at every turn with yourself—your selfish longings and self-absorbed acts. You have to start by seeking God, through prayer and worship and meditating on His Word.

God certainly wanted the people to pray. If they could submit to the Father in prayer, give up their wicked ways for a time to pray, if they could do all this, then God could hear them and forgive them and heal them.

God wants the same for you.

Dear Lord, help me to be humble, prayerful,
and ever seeking You. Amen. —ML

CANVAS

The heavens declare the glory of God;
the skies proclaim the work of his hands.
PSALM 19:1

Next time you cannot think of what words to pray, pick a warm day and find a soft, grassy field. Lie down on the bed of green and watch clouds swim across the ocean on high. Study the shades of blue as it changes from one end to the other. Look for where the sky meets the land on the horizon and wonder how far it must be to the ends of the world. Observe the birds winging their way high above you and imagine the delicate construction of their bones and feathers that allows them to transport themselves so easily for so far.

"The heavens declare the glory of God; the skies proclaim the work of his hands. Day after day they pour forth speech; night after night they reveal knowledge. They have no speech, they use no words; no sound is heard from them. Yet their voice goes out into all the earth, their words to the ends of the world" (vv. 1–4).

The heavens and skies declare God's glory like a painted canvas tells the ability of the artist. The canvas itself is not the art or skill. The skill of the painter is merely captured there for all to see.

When you have no words, be a canvas on which God's artistry can be revealed. The words will come later.

Dear Creator God, thank You for Your
amazing creations. Amen. —ML

THE HARD PRAYERS

"Will not the Judge of all the earth do right?"
GENESIS 18:25

What makes a question dangerous?

Some questions are dangerous because of the responses they require. "Do you love me?" Whatever reply is made to that question could change a person's life.

Some questions are dangerous because of what they might imply about the one who asks. "Do you love me?" could be met with "Why would you have to ask that?"

But you don't ever have to be afraid to ask a question of God. Some people go their whole lives, it seems, without ever asking God those pesky questions that have been a stumbling block to them for ages. It's easy to see why. It's frightening to face the King of kings with hard questions.

Yet God's been answering hard questions for centuries. Abraham wondered if a just God would kill both righteous and wicked together in order to destroy sinful cities. It was not just a question—it was a challenge: Are You truly a just judge, God? Who are You, anyway?

It's just a guess, but probably most of the hard questions people are afraid to bring up in prayer would fall into the categories of wanting to define who God is and why He does what He does. Is there anyone better to ask those questions of than God Himself?

*Dear God, give me courage to ask
You anything. Amen. —ML*

PEACEMAKING

*Therefore I want the men everywhere to pray,
lifting up holy hands without anger or disputing.*
1 TIMOTHY 2:8

There were lots of conflicting opinions about how things ought to be done. What kinds of ceremonies to perform and when, who should be in charge, what scripture calls for, what Jesus would have said or done—there were plenty of things to argue about.

Does this sound like any church you know?

The early church, just like churches today, was made up of people. Anytime you have human beings coming together over something as significant as the act of worshipping God, it's going to be a little messy. People at times have strong emotions, firmly held beliefs, and loud opinions—often all at once!—about their church.

Paul had told Timothy to stay at Ephesus for a reason. False teachers were sowing seeds of discord among the Christians there, promoting "controversial speculations rather than advancing God's work" (1 Timothy 1:4). Paul advised his friend to "fight the battle well" (v. 18), which gives us another clue as to the state of the Ephesian church at the time. Peace did not reign.

Prayer can be a peacemaker. If you can get two adversaries to stand and pray together, at the very least their hands will be stilled long enough not to come to blows. What's the mood of your church? Is there anyone that you need to stand in prayer with and come to peace?

Dear God, help me be a peacemaker. Amen. —ML

THE PRAYER OF SPECULATION

*A gossip betrays a confidence, but a
trustworthy person keeps a secret.*
PROVERBS 11:13

In some circles, the prayer line is known as the gossip train. Instead of being an act of love and care for our neighbors in trouble, the sharing of prayer concerns can become a time to talk freely about the private issues of friends and acquaintances, inserting judgments and drawing (most likely erroneous) conclusions along the way.

When does that line get crossed? There are several points of weakness in this fence, but here are a few. Anytime someone has shared a problem with you in confidence, whether that security is spelled out or implied, the sharing of that prayer stops with you and God. Unless you have been given permission to ask others to pray on the issue, word of it should go no further. Period.

If someone does ask you to deliver a request for prayer to others, do so as requested. But only as requested. Don't insert your own opinions or speculations. Don't drop hints or let your tone imply meaning that is not yours to give. Stick to the facts.

Being asked to lift someone's personal burdens up before our Father is a privilege. It was the duty of the priests of ancient times to do this for the people in the holy dwelling of God. Do not take this duty lightly. Be a trustworthy prayer partner.

*Dear God, guard my lips from slips that
could hurt others. Amen.* —ML

ASKING FOR IT

For what children are not disciplined by their father?
HEBREWS 12:7

It is a rare child indeed who loves discipline. There's something about the human will that balks at being told what to do. It does not matter who you are or how you were raised—this fact is true for everyone. Even very small children will often learn *no* as one of their first words.

Though not all earthly fathers deliver helpful instruction, we have no reason whatsoever to doubt that our heavenly Father's guidance will be "for our good, in order that we may share in his holiness" (v. 10). It may be hard. It may be annoying. It most certainly will not fit into our own plans. It may involve dealing with people we don't like or going places that make us uncomfortable. It may mean speaking out or shutting up. It will take a lot of listening. It will take a lot of work.

However painful it is at the time, we have to know it will be worth it. Our perfect Father has nothing but our good in mind. His view of that good is far purer and higher and deeper than what we could imagine.

So go ahead. Take the chance. Ask in prayer for God to discipline you. It's going to come someday anyway. You might as well get started!

Dear Father, train me in Your ways. Amen. —ML

SHAME

To you they cried out and were saved;
in you they trusted and were not put to shame.
PSALM 22:5

Shameless is one of those funny English words that mean the opposite of what they sound like. A shameless person is not, as it would seem, a person who has no reason to be shamed. Quite the contrary. A shameless person is one who has lived such a dishonorable life that she doesn't even have the ability to feel shame anymore.

The closer you are to God, the more likely you are to feel shame when you do wrong things. It is an honor to be a child of God and to have an intimate relationship with Him. Anything that hurts that relationship, especially because of your own doing, will make you feel the marring of that honor. And the more you desire God and spend time with Him, the more sensitive you will become to those little parts of your life that don't align with His will.

In some societies, shame and honor are equal to weakness and strength. In God's kingdom, we are made strong through our weakness. When we come to Him, cry out to Him, pray to Him, and submit to Him, we are saved. By humbling ourselves before Him and trusting in Him, we will not be put to shame but receive His honor instead.

Dear Lord, help me to be an honorable
child of Your kingdom. Amen. —ML

CALM

"Teacher, don't you care if we drown?"
MARK 4:38

The clouds rolled in, gray and heavy. The rain gradually gained speed and density. The formerly calm sea began churning. A large wave broke over the boat, flooding it and drenching everyone inside. The anxiety that had been growing on board reached a high point. Some of the men were fishermen; they were accustomed to stormy seas. But this storm was different. It had come on so suddenly and was so strong! The mysterious abyss seemed determined to either suck them in or burst them apart.

Men ran this way and that, trying to find ways to hold on, tying themselves to the boat, to each other, to anything they could grasp. People shouted directions to one another, trying to be helpful. Someone took a head count—making sure all the passengers were there. But one was missing. Where was Jesus?

They spotted Him, sleeping in the stern. Sleeping! In this squall? How could He? Why wasn't He helping them? Why wasn't He doing something? Didn't He care?

Have you ever asked God these questions in the middle of a personal storm?

The disciples found out that not only did Jesus care, but He had the ability to calm *their* cares all at once. "Quiet! Be still!"

He said it to the wind and the waves. He says it to us. Be still and know who is in the boat with us.

Dear God, help me to feel Your presence.
Please calm my fears. Amen. —ML

THE BURDEN
OF BEAUTY

*I have seen the burden God has laid on the human
race. He has made everything beautiful in its time.*
ECCLESIASTES 3:10–11

A starry night in the middle of a remote field. Mountains trimmed
with a golden sunrise. Crystal-blue waters dappled with light. A
perfectly formed rose. Tiny little fingernails on a tiny little newborn
hand. Flecks of gold joy in the irises of a loved one just before their
eyelids close a final time.

Have you ever been stunned by a moment, a vision so beautiful,
it took your breath away? Sometimes there are things too beautiful
to even try to describe, and there are thoughts that come to us that
feel too big to fit inside our minds.

The burden God has placed on us is also a gift—glimpses of
glory that hint at what is to come. They weigh heavily on us because
we have no box to contain them in, no way of grasping them. But
they also are the sweetest tastes of hope in heaven.

When you are caught by one of these moments—stop and pray.
Say thanks to God for the burden of beauty. Express your gratitude
for a momentary window into eternity. Perhaps one prayer at such
a time will be enough to help you hold on to that hope in less beautiful, darker days.

*Dear God, I cannot put into words how
great You are. Look into my heart and
see my love for You. Amen. —ML*

ON THE MAT

He is always wrestling in prayer for you,
that you may stand firm in all the will of
God, mature and fully assured.
COLOSSIANS 4:12

Praying for someone takes a lot of endurance. To follow a person through their ups and downs, successes and failures, can be emotionally exhausting, especially if you love that person very much. Thinking about them, asking God to guide them, hoping for them—it can all feel like a mental wrestling match.

But who are you wrestling with? Not the person at the center of your prayers—they might not even be aware of your efforts. Not God. This is no Jacob versus the angel story (see Genesis 32 for that account).

No, you are wrestling with yourself. With your own thoughts and worries about the person and how to ask God for help. Sometimes you might be wrestling with frustration at your inability to fix everything (because some things just won't be fixed that way). You might be wrestling with perseverance and patience in your prayers—struggling to hold on to hope for a person's life when it seems there's only a slim chance for things to get better. You might struggle to find the right requests to make on that person's behalf. You might fight with yourself to push down negative feelings such as bitterness, anger, and despair.

Engaging in the care and prayer for others can be a workout. But it's totally worth it.

Dear Lord, help me to persevere in my
prayers for others. Amen. —ML

WHO IS ABLE?

"Give your servant a discerning heart to govern your people and to distinguish between right and wrong."
1 KINGS 3:9

There's no doubt about it. If Solomon were to run for any high elected office today, he would win. He was wealthy. He was apparently not bad with wooing the ladies. Most of all, he was wise.

Wouldn't it be wonderful if every government official in our country today stopped what they were doing and just prayed this simple prayer of Solomon's? *Give me a discerning heart, God. Help me know the difference between what is right and what is wrong.* The earth might actually tremble if such an event happened.

Solomon's rhetorical question is apt today—"Who is able to govern this great people of yours?" (v. 9). Indeed. Who? It's a complex job, clouded by power, control, and a thousand other schemes the devil lays to ensnare the participants.

While we would like to think that things are more black and white, figuring out what is right or wrong to do as a governing body is quite difficult. Making a ruling for one person in one situation might not be so hard. But making a law that has to last and cover a multitude of possibilities, known and unknown, can be extremely complicated.

Pray for your nation's leaders. And ask them to be praying too—for discerning hearts and wise choices.

God, my King, pour out Your wisdom on the rulers of this nation. Amen. —ML

GIVING
GOOD GIFTS

*"Which of you fathers, if your son asks for
a fish, will give him a snake instead?"*
LUKE 11:11

It's probably not right to laugh at this scene, but can you imagine it? The little boy and his father are out on a campout, having some wonderful father-son bonding time together. They've been fishing all afternoon and the father has gathered their load to prepare some fish to cook over the fire for dinner. The boy is eager to taste the fruit of his labors and asks, "Hey Dad, can you pass me one of those fish?" His father tosses him a plate—full of rattlesnake!

Okay, maybe it wouldn't be so funny. But Jesus was making a point here by presenting the ridiculous. The crowd He was talking to would have gotten the joke—no honorable father would give his son gifts that would hurt him. A father in those times might well have been judged by the blessings bestowed on his children. The more prosperous and at ease his children appeared to be, the more respected the father would be.

So if mere human fathers are able to figure out how to give their children good things for dinner (even if it's just peanut butter sandwiches!), how much more ought we to trust God our Father to give us what we need?

Ask your Father for what you need. He will provide everything you ask, and much more.

Dear Father, fill me up with what I lack. Amen. —ML

ALL NATIONS

*"Who will not fear you, Lord,
and bring glory to your name?"*
REVELATION 15:4

If you began right now praying for one nation on earth every day, it would probably take you the better part of a year to finish the job. Estimates vary, and the status of nations vary as wars continue to be fought and political conditions change, but there are somewhere around two hundred different nations in this world. And if you count the different tribes living among those nations, the number grows even larger.

So many different people, so many different interests—can you imagine them all standing and giving glory to God? It seems impossible. But it also seems impossible that any people, no matter their background, could resist the awesome and majestic power of the almighty God.

Pray for the people living in nations where Christ is not preached. Pray that they might hear the gospel message in time to start living for Him. Pray for God's mercy and grace to be spread in cultures where fear and suffering still reign. Pray for whatever part you can have in delivering the message of love to those who are longing to hear it.

*Dear Lord, let me help in whatever way
I can to spread Your love and hope
to every nation. Amen. —ML*

NOT STOPPED

Since the day we heard about you,
we have not stopped praying for you.
COLOSSIANS 1:9

How do you feel when you learn that someone has been praying for you? *Grateful* is the word that springs to mind. What a gift to receive! To know that someone is remembering you and lifting your name up to God. It's one of the best things anyone could do for another person.

Scripture is not clear on who might be praying for us in heaven, though we know for certain Jesus intercedes for us. But it seems that if there's rejoicing in heaven when one sinner repents (Luke 15:10), then it's not unreasonable to think that quite a bit of praying is going on too.

Even now, someone in heaven might be lifting his voice and saying your name. Praying for you to be filled "with the knowledge of his will through all the wisdom and understanding that the Spirit gives, so that you may live a life worthy of the Lord and please him in every way" (Colossians 1:9–10). Someone might be praying for you to do good work, to learn well and acquire knowledge. Someone might be asking for God's power to make you strong and able to endure all things. Someone might be joyfully thanking our Father in heaven, just because you were born and you are a member of God's family.

Someone, somewhere, is praying for you. Aren't you glad?

Dear Lord, help me be faithful in my
prayers for others. Amen. —ML

SOLITUDE

Very early in the morning, while it was still
dark, Jesus got up, left the house and went
off to a solitary place, where he prayed.
MARK 1:35

Where do you pray? Do you pray in a busy office, coffee in one hand and papers clenched in another? Do you pray as you scrub each finger outside the operating room, just before surgery begins? Do you pray at your desk, when the students in front of you are taking a test? Do you pray in the relative quiet of your locked bathroom, while a toddler knocks persistently on the other side?

It's strangely comforting to know that the Prince of Peace needed quiet times too. Really quiet times. Away from people. Away even from the house where people might be. Somewhere alone, still, dark. A solitary place.

We need those quiet times too. Time to focus on the Lord alone and not be distracted by what is going on around us. Certainly, it's not something that can happen on every day of the week. You have to plan for it. You may even have to get up very early in the morning. But it's important to find time, every once in a while, when it can be just you and God together. No one else. No rush. Nowhere to be. Nothing else to do.

Make plans to find your solitary place today.

Dear Lord, I need time alone with You.
Help me to make that happen. Amen. —ML

ENDLESS POSSIBILITIES

"For where two or three gather in my name, there am I with them."
MATTHEW 18:20

In our society, individual success is glorified over the benefits of a group of people working together. But if you've ever met a fund-raising goal, run a race, or completed a service project with a group, you know how fantastic it can be. To see people with different gifts join those together as one unit is a beautiful thing. It can be frustrating too. The fact that it isn't always a piece of cake makes the accomplishment that much sweeter. When you are finished, you feel pride not just in the work of your own hands but in the group as a whole. Nothing seems impossible to do if you could gather enough people willing to work together.

Jesus confirms this feeling: "If two of you on earth agree about anything they ask for, it will be done" (v. 19). Does this mean that anything we pray for together we will receive? Maybe. Certainly if Jesus says the Father will do it, then the Father will. However, God is not limited by our human designs, so how a thing gets "done" for us by the Father may look a bit different from what we had in mind. Sometimes it might even look worse. Yet the end result will no doubt be infinitely better than what we could imagine.

Dear Lord, thank You for living
life with us. Amen. —ML

NUDGES

"Speak, LORD, for your servant is listening."
1 SAMUEL 3:9

It may be a passing memory. You think of an old friend and wonder how they are. Maybe it's a burst of inspiration. You suddenly see the solution to a problem that has been a struggle for others. It could come as a twinge of guilt. You feel you should go to someone and apologize.

The call was plain in 1 Samuel 3, but even then Samuel didn't recognize it right away. It took three times of being woken up in the middle of the night by the boy before old Eli put two and two together. He realized it was the Lord, so he told the boy to lie down again. Then, if Samuel should hear the voice calling his name again, Eli told him to answer, "Speak, LORD, for your servant is listening."

Most of us would have probably told Samuel to just ignore the voice and go to sleep, for goodness' sake. After all, isn't that what we tell ourselves?

We get a nudge from God. It comes as a whisper, a thought, a glimpse, a passing idea—maybe even a dream. We wave it away. We shrug it off. We ignore the voice.

Next time you have a thought or feeling that comes out of the blue, consider that it might not be coming out of nowhere. It might be coming from the heavenly Father.

Speak, Lord. I am listening. Amen. —ML

PROTECTION, NOT ISOLATION

"My prayer is not that you take them out of the world but that you protect them from the evil one."
JOHN 17:15

Through the centuries of the history of the church, there have been groups of people who came to the conclusion that the only way to stay faithful was to isolate themselves from the evils of this world. So that's exactly what they did. And the extent to which this plan was successful or not could be debated (though there's not room for that here).

But that doesn't seem to be the plan Jesus had for us. In His wonderful, revealing prayer of John 17, Jesus asked God not to "take them out of the world" (*them* referring to "those whom you gave me out of the world" [v. 6]) but to give the people protection from the evil one. Jesus Himself states that, along with being "not of the world," He was indeed sent "into the world" (vv. 16, 18).

Jesus did not isolate Himself. When He was on the earth, He was walking among the people. He was living and eating and sleeping with the people, not in some fortress on His own.

We are supposed to love one another. It's hard to do that very well from behind a wall. So if you have built up barriers between you and "the world," it may be time to break those down. Don't be afraid. Ask God for help, and He will protect you.

God, help me to reach others for You. Amen. —ML

EVEN NOW

*"But I know that even now God will
give you whatever you ask."*
JOHN 11:22

Jesus loved Martha and Mary and Lazarus. It says so right in the Bible. Those three seemed to have a special relationship with the Lord. So it's natural that when their brother became sick, the sisters sent word to Jesus.

What do you want Jesus to do when someone you love is sick and dying?

If you've ever had the sorrow of having to wait by the bedside while someone you love is in the last stages of life, you probably know the heaviness of that experience. You start to reach in your mind for any possibility, any solution, and any chance at all to change the final outcome.

Have you ever sent word to Jesus about a friend or family member? "Jesus, the one You love is sick." "Jesus, please come." "Jesus, please heal him." "Jesus, please don't let her die."

The God who formed you in the womb and shaped you into the being you now are knows the plan for your life, including its end. As hard as it might be to understand at the time, He is with us, even in that final chapter.

When Martha spoke to Jesus after her brother's death, she declared her faith. "I know that even now God will give you whatever you ask."

Do you know God is with you, even now?

*Dear Lord, I am not ready to let go. Help me
believe You are with me to the end. Amen. —ML*

PRAYERS OF THE WEAK

For when I am weak, then I am strong.
2 CORINTHIANS 12:10

People have made different guesses as to what the "thorn" in Paul's flesh might have been. But it doesn't really matter what it was. All we need to know—all the Corinthians needed to know—is that it was something that made him feel significantly weakened. He was tormented by it—so much so that he pleaded with God to get rid of it.

What is your thorn? What's the weak spot in your armor?

Thank God today for your weaknesses. Thank Him for the times when you've had to rely on Him alone. Thank Him for the days when nothing went your way. Thank God for your failures and your falters.

For when you didn't have it all together, you had to lean on God. You had to see He was the only way out. You had to know only He could give you the resources you needed. You had to believe His words: "My grace is sufficient for you, for my power is made perfect in weakness" (v. 9).

When you have lost your strength, take a moment to be glad for God's grace and to give Him the glory.

Dear Jesus, thank You for making Your power and my need for You abundantly clear. Amen. —ML

MY ROCK

Truly my soul finds rest in God; my salvation comes
from him. Truly he is my rock and my salvation;
he is my fortress, I will never be shaken.
PSALM 62:1–2

Imagine the crashing waves of the sea. They grab at the grains of
sand and swirl them away, changing the very shape of the land.
Walking through the sand is difficult. There is no sure foothold. Your
feet slip and get stuck. You stumble. You fall.

Then you reach a big rock. You climb up onto the top of it,
and from here you can see the crashing waves running toward you.
You tap your foot on the rock below you—solid. No crumbling, no
shifting. This foundation isn't going anywhere.

God is our rock. He is the place on which we can stand firm.
He is the power by which we can hold tight to our faith. He is the
hope in which we can rest securely, knowing we will not be swept
away in the end.

It is hard to walk in a world where the rules keep changing, where
the values of what is right and what is important seem to flip every
day. We can be sure our God will not change, and what He tells us
will always be true. In that truth, we can find rest.

Dear God, thank You for being my rock! Amen. —ML

HEALTHY FRUIT

*We constantly pray for you, that our God may
make you worthy of his calling, and that by his
power he may bring to fruition your every desire for
goodness and your every deed prompted by faith.*

2 THESSALONIANS 1:11

The process of growing fruit can be rewarding, but it also takes time and lots of care. First a plant has to mature and become capable of producing seeds. Then the blossoms of the plant have to be pollinated and fertilized. The plant produces seeds, protected by the fruit of the plant and ready to travel to make new plants grow.

We are like fruit trees in God's orchard. He makes us grow. Through the discipline of faith, through prayer and reading of God's Word, and through His love, we mature and become able to influence others and teach others about Christ. We plant seeds of the gospel in the world and protect them with prayer and through the acts we do in faith.

Through our growth and the spreading of seeds, we have to be protected from the diseases of wickedness and despair that plague our world. We have to stay firmly rooted in God and in the family of believers in order to continue to grow and produce fruit that will be complete and healthy.

So we constantly pray for each other, that we may be made worthy for God's harvest.

*Dear Lord, thank You for every day I
can grow in You. Amen.* —ML

MERCY

*He saved us, not because of righteous things
we had done, but because of his mercy.*
Titus 3:5

People can get and have gotten into all kinds of heated arguments over how a person actually gets "saved." Is it through baptism by immersion? Is it through the Spirit? Is it through words? Is it through faith?

The truth is it is none of those things without the generous mercy of our Lord God. We are saved from a permanent death and have access to eternal life through the grace of Jesus Christ our Savior alone. Nothing we do, no ceremony, no spoken words, no promises made—no one can save us except Jesus. Had He not given His life on the cross and conquered the grave, we could say a thousand prayers or dunk ourselves a million different ways and we would still be separated from God for eternity.

But through this gift of grace, we are justified and we are saved "through the washing of rebirth and renewal by the Holy Spirit" (v. 5). Through this we have the hope of eternal life.

So, as Paul stressed, the point is to understand mercy, so we can be careful to devote ourselves to the right things—to doing what is good, for each other and for God.

*Dear Lord, help me be an encourager to anyone
who claims You as their Savior. Amen. —ML*

A MASTERPIECE
IN THE MAKING

*For we are God's handiwork, created in
Christ Jesus to do good works, which God
prepared in advance for us to do.*
EPHESIANS 2:10

When people see a hunk of wood or stone or clay or metal, they might see no more than junk. Something unusable, even ugly. But to a gifted artist, well, she sees something else.

Potential.

She knows how to take a piece of wood and give it new life—perhaps by carving a seagull in flight or a beautiful fruit bowl or a child playing a flute. She can make a treasure. A keepsake.

God is the master artist, and in us He sees all the potential. We are His "handiwork," created in Christ Jesus to do good works. We are not junk or ugly or unusable, as the enemy of our souls would like us to believe. Those are lies, and we must never believe them. Instead know that God is ready to mold and shape us into a work of art. It might take a bit of time—and it might be painful at times—but it will be worth it.

Pray that God will begin the process of carving something beautiful out of your life. That you will be a masterpiece in the making.

*Father, mold and shape me into a brilliant display of
Your likeness. I want to reflect the many facets of Your
character to those I encounter. Make me malleable to
Your touch and receptive to Your voice. Amen. —AH*

THE SPIRIT OF TRUTH

"But when he, the Spirit of truth, comes, he will guide you into all the truth. He will not speak on his own; he will speak only what he hears, and he will tell you what is yet to come."
JOHN 16:13

If you've ever been hiking, you know that there are some common-sense guidelines that will help to keep you safe—such as hiking with a buddy, taking a good map, wearing comfortable boots that are broken in, and taking plenty of water, just to name a few. Ignoring good hiking rules can lead to treacherous circumstances.

And just as in hiking, ignoring the good biblical guidelines that God has put before us can also be deadly. The Lord and His powerful Word are our travel guides as we journey through this dangerous passageway we call life. Without our Savior, the daily jungle gets dark and scary, and all the trails will eventually lead to destruction.

With Christ as our guide, we can feel secure, since He promises to guide us into all truth. He will watch over our comings and goings. He will show us the right course to follow here on earth and the pathway to eternal life through Christ.

Pray daily that the Lord and His living Word will be our holy guide, since His way is not just a good way to go—it's the only right way.

Holy Spirit, give me daily direction and purpose. Help me to remain within Your light and truth. Amen. —AH

I AM WITH
YOU ALWAYS

"Do not let your hearts be troubled.
You believe in God; believe also in me."
JOHN 14:1

From the moment we emerge from our mother's womb, squalling and red and upset, until we breathe our last breath, our hearts are burdened with troubles of every kind. We know loneliness, disappointment, and pain so deep that it scorches our very souls. What relief is there for us when all humans fail us—friends, doctors, family members, counselors, and sometimes even pastors?

Jesus takes us to a quiet place, and He speaks to us. He tells us that we are very dear to Him. We are His friends—His beloved children. When we fall, He picks us up. When we fail, He restores our souls. When we get discouraged, He lifts us up. When we are lost, His hand is ever near. When we walk in the darkest valleys of this life journey, burdened with many cares, He helps us carry our load. He is our strength. He is our fortress. He is all we need.

Jesus comforted His disciples with the words "Do not let your hearts be troubled. You believe in God; believe also in me." As we pray, He will speak those same words to me and to you if we listen with an earnest heart.

"Dear one, be not troubled. I am here."

Lord Jesus, I give to You the burdens of my
heart. I cast my anxiety onto You because
I know that You care for me—more than I
could possibly imagine. Amen. —AH

HOW DO
I LOVE GOD?

Jesus replied: " 'Love the Lord your God with all your heart and with all your soul and with all your mind.' This is the first and greatest commandment."
MATTHEW 22:37–38

If you love your mom and dad—hopefully you do—do they know it? Really know it, all the way to the depths of their hearts? Do you say the words "I love you" often to them, or are you neglectful, hoping that saying it on birthdays and holidays is enough? Do you show your love for them in your actions?

Showing God that we love Him has some similarities to loving our parents. If we love the Lord with all our heart and soul and mind, does He know it? Or are we neglectful in saying, "I love You"? Do we show our love for Jesus within our actions? Do we relish spending time with Him? The Lord cherishes our fellowship, and He hopes for our love and devotion as well.

Other ways to show God that we love Him would be through other gifts of the heart, such as repentance, respect, obedience, and thanksgiving. This can be our grateful response to His great love, His daily tender mercies, and His abundant grace.

How will you show the Lord today that you love Him? What will you say?

Heavenly Father, I love You. Thank You for first loving me. Help me to show my love for You through my lifestyle and attitude. Amen. —AH

THIS
QUIET MEADOW

"Peace I leave with you; my peace I give you.
I do not give to you as the world gives."
JOHN 14:27

There's a sunlit meadow with your name on it. You are daily drawn to that haven like a butterfly to a blousy ripe blossom. There in that golden meadow, the breeze is summer silk, and the clouds come in fanciful shapes like plush toys in a child's playroom. You stroll through the grasses and leisurely gather a bouquet of wild roses. You brush the velvet petals against your cheek as you breathe in.

Then, naturally—wanting to thank someone for this glimpse of heaven—you raise your gaze and thank the Lord of all. His company is warm and welcoming like the sun. You stroll together in sweet devotion, and you drink in the splendorous peace that only a cup of His presence can provide. He is yours. You are His. Your spirit smiles in response.

Hmm. Sound far-fetched? Yes, this scenario is impossible in a world that raises the flags of hurry, fear, and confusion while it marches to the motto of "Yes, you can have it all, do it all—now!"

Jesus takes us on a different journey. He leads us to fragrant meadows and quiet streams. For intimate communion. For peace—His peace—that passes all understanding. Such divine companionship is ours.

Can't you hear Him now? There is this quiet meadow, and He's calling your name.

My dear Lord, help me to find quiet
fellowship with You even amid the rush
and panic of life. Amen. —AH

207

ISN'T IT
ALL ABOUT ME?

"For even the Son of Man did not come to be served, but to serve, and to give his life as a ransom for many."
MARK 10:45

The world screams, "Look at me!" while the Lord whispers, "I came as a servant."

Uh-oh.

That word *servant* doesn't jive very well with today's "all about me" mindset. The concept of being a servant is as chic as wearing a dirty apron over a designer gown. Not a fashion look that would make it to a New York runway, eh?

We don't like to think of ourselves as anything but on the top of the human heap—mistresses of our own destinies—while servanthood appears to be at the bottom and might include the unpopular words of *sacrifice* and *suffering*. Certainly, the life of Christ was filled with both sacrifice and suffering. Of course, the price for our sins has already been paid in full, so we can add nothing to Jesus' death on the cross, but to have the heart of a servant is honorable. This choice will be rewarded—perhaps not in this life but in the one to come.

Let us pray that we can understand these divine mysteries and that God will give us the courage to tread along this most noble and beautiful footpath—that of being a servant of Jesus Christ.

Savior, thank You for showing me the true meaning of servanthood. Teach me how to place others before myself. Amen. —AH

IT MAY
HAPPEN LIKE THIS

You, LORD, keep my lamp burning;
my God turns my darkness into light.
PSALM 18:28

That nighttime routine with your child may happen like this: You've spent the last hour trying unsuccessfully to get little Penelope to go to sleep. First is a story, then a glass of water. Then she needs an extra hug. Then she wants to go to the bathroom. When all is finally as quiet as a sleepy mouse, you tiptoe away.

Then comes the big howling cry, "There's a monster under my bed!" What do you do? You talk away her fears, say a prayer, and kiss her forehead.

Haven't you too been afraid of the dark? Those times you felt more comfortable singing when passing through a dark passage? Or the times you rushed to a light switch and you felt such a surge of relief when the light came on? With God by our side there is no reason to fear the dark, or the enemy, or anything the world can do to us. Those words in Psalm 18 are so comforting, aren't they? The Lord will keep our lamp burning brightly, and He will turn our darkness into light!

The Lord's light can never be diminished, and that light is brighter than any sun, more holy than any other being, and more beautiful than anything we have ever known.

When we pray, we step into that holy light. What do we have to fear?

Lord, You are the source of all light
and all that is good. Bring me into Your
holy presence. Amen. —AH

KNOW
MY HEART

Search me, God, and know my heart;
test me and know my anxious thoughts.
See if there is any offensive way in me,
and lead me in the way everlasting.
PSALM 139:23–24

If you know anything about rodents, you know they like to run and hide in dark corners. They don't generally come out and present themselves in the bright light.

Sometimes our hearts are so full of wrongdoing that we tend to have a few rodent-like habits of our own. When our actions and thoughts are not so holy, we hope they aren't placed under a spotlight.

In Psalm 139, it encourages us to do the opposite. We should ask God to search our souls, to know us intimately, to test us and know even our worries. We are to take it a step further and ask Him if there is any offensive way in us and to lead us in the way everlasting.

This biblical directive and divine scrutiny doesn't sound easy, since to voluntarily step into His light to be judged isn't on the top of our list of fun things to do. We are deeply concerned that He will find some offensive ways in us.

Perhaps one could ponder the scripture in this light—wouldn't it be better to endure the Lord's discipline and become faithful and lovely in spirit than to enjoy the evil applause of Satan and lose our very souls?

How shall we then pray?

Holy Spirit, please break down the walls around
my heart and sweep out the dusty, dark places that
harbor sin, bitterness, and distrust. Amen. —AH

BE INSPIRED!

"You alone are the LORD. You made the heavens, even the highest heavens, and all their starry host, the earth and all that is on it, the seas and all that is in them. You give life to everything, and the multitudes of heaven worship you."
NEHEMIAH 9:6

When you wake up each morning, know that the one in charge is not only the Maker of all but a lavish and mystifying and beautifully beguiling Creator being.

His works stir our souls. Reach out to us. Embrace us. Delight us. Surprise us. He crafts such magnificent objects that we cannot replicate them or even fully understand them, such as the mysteries of frost flowers, the northern lights, glowing plankton, moonbows, meat-eating plants, and red lightning—just to name a very few.

To think, we are made in His image—the one who created all the wonders of the earth—including you and me. We too have that imprint on us—that passion to create. We have the need to interact with the one who gave us those gifts. Jesus came to give us that connection to our Creator. Jesus came to give us eternal life, and abundant life, which includes time spent with Him in creating marvels.

What can you create with God today as Father and daughter? Not *for* Him, but *with* Him as collaborators in this supernatural dance? Just ask Him, "Father, what can we do today?"

Creator God, You are truly awesome and inspiring. Thank You for the ability to create. Amen. —AH

HUMBLE PIE

For by the grace given me I say to every one
of you: Do not think of yourself more highly
than you ought, but rather think of yourself
with sober judgment, in accordance with the
faith God has distributed to each of you.
ROMANS 12:3

Have you ever witnessed this scene? A woman strolls into a party, nose in the air, purse swinging wide with a bigheaded sashay that would put a rock star to shame. She knows who she is, what she's about, and exactly what she wants. If you even think about getting in her way, you might need a trip to the emergency room.

The letter to the Romans says we are not to think too highly of ourselves. We are instead to judge ourselves with thoughtful discernment and wisdom. That doesn't mean we should despise ourselves. Not at all. We are children of the living God. We should never think that we alone are conquerors of anything without the help of the Almighty.

Pray that the Lord will give us a meek and pleasing attitude in His sight and that we will conduct ourselves with an unassuming spirit in all situations.

After all, it would be better to sit at a lowly place at the table and be regarded with esteem than to rush ahead and sit at the head of the table, only to be forced to eat a large portion of humble pie.

Dear Lord Jesus, help me to view myself
through honest eyes, mindful of my flaws and
reliant on You to change me. Amen. —AH

A SINGLE RAY
OF SUNLIGHT

*"In the same way, let your light shine before
others, that they may see your good deeds
and glorify your Father in heaven."*
MATTHEW 5:16

If you've ever strolled through a lovely forest, you know how delightful it can be to come across a lone tree that is lit by a single ray of sunlight. What a heavenly surprise—as if the angels had parted the canopy of branches so that the sun could illuminate that one solitary spot. The leaves on the tree seem to glow from within. The place seems almost sacred somehow. What a wonderful, serendipitous moment to pause and ponder its beauty. What a wonderful moment to praise God.

We as Christians should be like that light before men. There should be an illumination on our faces that comes from within, and our good deeds should glorify God, so that people are drawn to that beauty and light. In other words, we should be that irresistible glow that shines in a dark wood. So that people feel compelled to pause along their journey to ponder the Christ we reflect, and so they might come to know that light in their own hearts.

Wouldn't that be an ideal prayer in the morning—that we, with the help of the Holy Spirit, could be that heavenly surprise to someone? That we could be that glow of Christ in someone else's life?

*Jesus, help me to reflect that irresistible glow in
a world that needs Your light. Amen. —AH*

THE BEST DAY OF YOUR LIFE

However, as it is written: "What no eye has seen, what no ear has heard, and what no human mind has conceived"—the things God has prepared for those who love him.

1 CORINTHIANS 2:9

When you were a kid, what was one of the best days of your life? Maybe you picked wildflowers for your mom, and after you handed them to her, she gave you a big hug. Or you went fishing with your dad and caught the biggest fish imaginable. Or you baked cookies with your grandma. Most likely those family memories bring a smile to your face and give a tug to your heartstrings.

Our heavenly Father would also like to interact with us in family fellowship. He'd like to be with us in what we do and where we go, whether it is to hike a trail or build a house or catch a fish or bake some cookies or sail a ship or pick a bouquet of wildflowers. God says that we cannot even conceive of all the wonderful things He has planned for those who love Him. We should wake up with a spirit of great expectation of wonderful things and with the joy of knowing the Lord loves us so much that He wants to share in all those experiences with us.

So, take His hand, hold on tight, and go—have the best day of your life!

Father God, help me not to lose sight of the joy, freedom, peace, and strength that is to be found in a relationship with You. Amen. —AH

HOW TO
KNOW CHRIST

*For God so loved the world that he gave his
one and only Son, that whoever believes in
him shall not perish but have eternal life.*

JOHN 3:16

Sometimes people can go a lifetime without praying the most important, powerful, and life-changing prayer of all. Maybe they've cried out to God in a crisis, but they've never really walked with Him or accepted Him as their Redeemer.

We can feel in our souls that this world is hurt and broken and that we are utterly lost. Yet there is hope. This spiritual answer—the only one that is true or lasting—is the redemption that comes from Jesus Christ.

If you haven't prayed the prayer of salvation, what keeps you from it? Despair? Pride? Lies from the enemy? If so, ask the Holy Spirit to lead you to the truth and for a softening of the heart. He will not fail you.

*And when you're ready, pray with an earnest
heart, "Lord Jesus, I admit that I have sinned.
I cannot save myself. I acknowledge You, Jesus,
as the Son of God—the only way to heaven—and
as the Lord and Savior of my life. Please come
to live in me and make me all that I was meant
to be. Thank You for Your sacrifice on the cross
and Your saving grace. I praise You for Your
goodness and mercy and life everlasting. Help
me to love You and follow You all the days of
my life. In Jesus' name I pray. Amen." —AH*

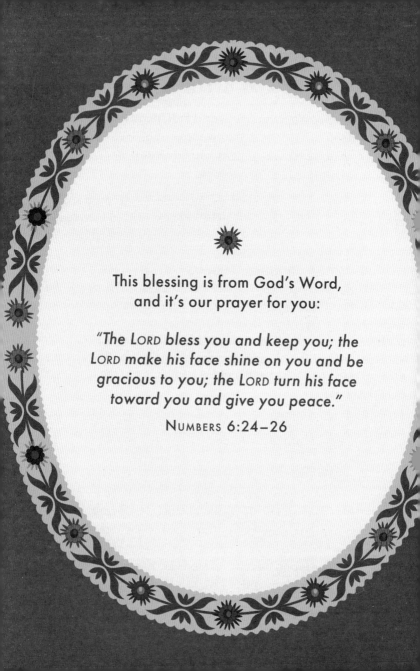

This blessing is from God's Word,
and it's our prayer for you:

"The LORD bless you and keep you; the
LORD make his face shine on you and be
gracious to you; the LORD turn his face
toward you and give you peace."

NUMBERS 6:24–26